Jack

Jack

by

Ann Hiorns-Neale

**COOPER
BOOKS**

Photographic acknowledgments

Front cover and front inside flap – Ann Hiorns-Neale
Back inside flap – author's father
Back cover 'Jack on Harlech beach' – Ann Hiorns-Neale
No.1 Carol Storey
Nos.2,4-7,10,13,14,20-30 Ann Hiorns-Neale
Nos.3,18,19 Eric James
Nos.8,11 Malcolm Donley
Nos.9,15 Dick Richards
Nos.12,16,17,31,32 Mark Hiorns-Neale

ISBN 0-9550125-0-3

Published by Cooper Books,
P.O. Box 44,
Felbrigg,
Norwich,
NR11 8WZ

Printed in England
by Bidnall Press Limited,
Beccles,
Suffolk, NR34 7TD

This book is dedicated to the memory of Jack
who got so much out of life
and gave me so much in life

To a Black Greyhound

Shining black in the shining light,
Inky black in the golden sun,
Graceful as the swallows flight,
Light as swallow, winged one,
Swift as driven hurricane –
Double-sinewed stretch and spring,
Muffled thud of flying feet,
See the black dog galloping,
Hear his wild foot-beat.

See him lie when day is dead,
Black curves curled on boarded floor.
Sleepy eyes, my sleepy-head –
Eyes that were aflame before.
Gentle now, they burn no more;
Gentle now and softly warm,
With the fire that made them bright
Hidden – as when after storm
Softly falls the night.

By Julian Grenfell (1888 – 1915)

Contents

Introduction

This book is first and foremost aimed at owners of retired greyhounds. It is a biographical account of Jack's life with me, taken from diaries and memory, covering Jack's initial wild and stubborn ways; how I coped with what he threw at me; some of the people and dogs we met, and Jack's behaviour with these dogs; dominance; dog behaviour; Jack's character and his great sense of humour; his escapades; how he progressed and calmed down; and the love that grew between us.

Although it is an account of Jack's life with me, it is also written with a view of being helpful and informative to other retired greyhound owners, who may learn from my experiences and will recognise some of Jack's traits and actions, in their greyhound(s), which will help them understand that what their dog does, and why it does it, is normal for a retired greyhound.

With regard to the occasional mention of Jack 'having a wee', it is not through some strange fetish on my part but to show part of Jack's character. Uncastrated males don't urinate because they need to empty their bladder – apart from when they have been prevented from doing so for some considerable time – they do so to mark an area with their scent and as part of a display of body language. So, mentioning Jack 'leaving a sprinkling of wee', is to show that he was making a statement. And he certainly liked to make his feelings known!

Most greyhounds settle in quickly and are open and friendly, desiring your attention and giving their love freely. Jack wasn't typical of a greyhound – he had a unique character, which I hope comes across in the book and that others may share in the enjoyment that he brought into my life.

CHAPTER 1

The Arrival

When my first greyhound, Jim, had to be put to sleep at the age of fourteen and a half years, I was adamant that I wasn't going to have another dog. Five years passed before I moved down to East Anglia for a job. Living and working on a large country estate, consisting of 500 acres of woodland and around 1200 acres of parkland, I thought to myself, "Jim would have loved it here."

In the meantime, I met and married Mark who also worked on the estate. Sometimes I talked to Mark about Jim and greyhounds in general and we started to notice just how many lived in our area. When I lost my job due to a back injury, we contemplated getting a greyhound. This contemplation soon became a burning desire for both of us and our search began.

For some reason, I was determined on a black male but a small one. Everywhere we went to look, the dogs were too big or not black. Eventually, I heard of one that had just retired and I was put in touch with the trainer. We arranged a meeting one Saturday in October 1999. Previous to this, we had completely fenced-in the garden to make it escape-proof, as we knew a greyhound would be coming along sooner or later.

On the Friday before, we decided to make room at home, just in case we brought him back. Frenzied activity ensued, surprising us in how much space one can create or how ruthless one can be in discarding long-kept, useless objects, when something is so important. Room was made in the cubby-hole for dog food and room for a bed, in the living room. Not that we had a bed; a folded blanket with a sheepskin on top would make do at first. Bed came late and knowledge of an early start, combined with anticipation, made sleep difficult.

At six a.m. we reluctantly parted from our warm duvet; washing, dressing, emptying the ashes from the Rayburn and breakfasting. With maps and directions, we climbed into the Land Rover by eight a.m. expecting a two-hour journey. With no mistakes and sticking to speed restrictions, it took us three and a half hours.

Arriving in the remotest place imaginable, kennel blocks and caged runs stretching as far as the eye could see, this kennel housed over ninety dogs and even had its own training track.

A kennel boy was sent to fetch Jimmy, the dog, who almost dragged the boy along and only stopped to cock his leg on the nearest thing, which happened to be Mark, who was squatting down at the time. So off to a good start then.

The lead was handed to us and I proceeded to look the dog over. His teeth were in an appalling state, encrusted with plaque but he had a good scissor bite. He wasn't cow-hocked or knock-kneed, had a good head, a beautiful long tail and strong upright toes yet wasn't interested in us one little bit. Staring hard into the distance, he was looking for whatever he had come out to chase.

We were invited to take him for a walk along the riverbank and boy, was he strong. This did not bother me, as I knew he would soon get used to walking normally on the lead. What did concern me was his apparent unwillingness to acknowledge Mark or myself. He didn't seem to like being stroked and would wrench his head out of the way of our touch. I thought his ears were awful, pricked so upright that they almost crossed each other, which then gave him a frown.

What made me agree to take him, I'll never know. The trainer said that if the dog didn't work out, we could not return him. I suddenly realised what an unknown quantity the dog was; we had no idea how he would turn out. He had just turned four and had raced for two years, eight months, his last race being ten days previous.

The first problem surfaced pretty quickly. He would not jump into the back of the Land Rover, so Mark had to lift him in. The heavens opened as we set off and Jack, as I had named him, whined and panted like a steam engine the whole time, misting every window to oblivion.

On the way, we stopped to pick up some dog food and to take Jack a little walk. When it came to getting him into the Land Rover, we opened the back door and I ran with Jack, so that he had to jump or crash into the rear of the vehicle. He jumped. We had to stop again, in town, so we took Jack with us. He was very willing and eager to see all things new to him and coped very well with the bustling crowds. When it came time to put him in the Land Rover again and I ran him towards the back, he knew what was expected of him and stopped short, refusing to jump in. Once again, Mark had to lift Jack into the vehicle. On our leaving the kennels, I had been handed a bowl containing his meal for that day. I decided to feed him at this moment, as it was way past his normal mealtime and he must be very hungry.

On arriving home, Jack tentatively explored the ground floor of our house, delicately sniffing furniture and carpets; inspecting everything minutely. We decided a bath was necessary, as he had a small amount of flea dirt and smelt of kennels, although the kennel he had come from was exceptionally clean, with mountains of shredded paper for bedding. We opened one of the doors to the stairs and with Jack on the lead, to make sure of no accidents as he had never previously encountered stairs, we ascended slowly at first, ending with a rush. He volunteered to enter the bathroom to investigate, so we closed the door and ran the water, placing a long rubber mat in the bath to prevent Jack from slipping. He didn't seem too bothered as we rubbed in the insecticidal shampoo although as time went on, he became impatient and fidgety, leaning against Mark's head and shoulder and nearly sliding over.

Pleased to be lifted onto dry land again, Jack shook himself thoroughly from his nose to the tip of his long tail, drenching Mark and I, along with everything else in the bathroom, as I rubbed him with a towel. As we cleared up, he trotted about the landing, glancing down the stairs now and again, knowing that we had come up that way, so we had to go down that way but it looked a bit tricky.

We were ready to go. I went down a few stairs then turned to face Jack, encouraging him. Shaking all over, he put one paw on the first stair down, then retracted it and tried the other one. Backing off and coming forward again, he just could not find the courage to head downwards. Mark carried him. We hoped his fear of stairs would prevent him from wanting to go up to the first floor.

We showed Jack his 'bed' and he lay down straight away, seeming to know it was for him. Every noise was followed closely as he tried to work out what it was, pricking his ears and tilting his head from side to side. He also whined frequently, in various tones and pitches, looking totally lost and unhappy.

When we made our tea and carried the food through into the living room, Jack danced excitedly around us, thinking it was for him and trying his best to fight his way to our dishes on the coffee table. A few stern "No's" confused him, until a rolled-up TV paper skimmed the end of his nose, when he thought it most appropriate to retire to his bed. This went on for a few nights. We soon realised Jack was a very determined dog.

Mark took him for a walk before bedtime and on his return, we went upstairs closing the door behind us, leaving Jack downstairs. He was most upset, whining and barking while we went to the toilet, did our teeth and got into bed. When he started howling, I decided to go down to talk to him through the door. Every time he tuned up, I said a stern, "NO," which quieted him for a short while. Eventually he settled down and so did we.

Around three a.m., I awoke to hear what I knew to be the sound of a dog vomiting. Down I went to clear up and to stay with Jack. He had done some diarrhoea on newspaper I had put down on the kitchen floor for him. The next day, he cocked his leg on the cooker, so I tapped his thigh, saying, "NO," and "outside" and also, "in the garden," whilst opening the back door. Out he went to cock his leg on a bush instead and never fouled indoors again. I was much relieved to find that Jack seemed to have no desire to destroy anything as well as being house-trained in five minutes.

That day, Sunday, we walked down to the unveiling of our new village sign. Quite a number of people were gathered on and around the green, some wanting to say hello to Jack. He coped well but wasn't keen on the children. After a speech or two, the veil came off the sign and we all applauded. Jack very nearly pulled out of his collar, rearing up and backing off. After a second bout of clapping, he had had enough and backed off when anyone approached. We thought it wise to leave and walked back through woodland and over the parkland. For a few weeks, he was very nervous of people unless they had a dog with them, otherwise he would refuse to go near them. He would trot round our garden at a fast pace, as if looking for a way out so he could find his way back to the kennels and his racing. When he did this, he looked extremely stressed, so I would take him indoors where he would whine and whine, trying to tell me what was wrong, which was pretty stressing for me too.

A trip to the vets was organised, for a thorough check-over and we wondered how Jack would react in a room full of people and dogs. The first thing we met outside the entrance was the tiniest bitch I had seen which, to our great relief, he greeted with a wagging tail and sniffs. Inside, he met a young Labrador that he was overjoyed to acquaint himself with. Jack was given a clean bill of health, except for his teeth; an appointment being made for a complete scale a week later.

I couldn't move without being shadowed by Jack; he didn't do this with Mark. In fact, he would bark at Mark each lunchtime and evening, when Mark came home from work. If I wanted to go upstairs, my telling Jack to, "stay there," had no effect whatsoever and he would struggle to force his way through the door, to see where I was going and to make sure he wasn't left alone. He was so incredibly strong; I would be trying to push him back and he would be desperately trying to push through me, hurting himself and squeaking out. I usually won in the end but felt exhausted yet amazed at his sheer determination.

When Mark was at home one day, I decided to let Jack come upstairs to explore and to see each room, so he would know how far we humans could disappear to. He didn't miss his chance. He was through the open door like greased lightening and up fourteen stairs in three bounds. He stood looking down at us, waving his tail, appearing very pleased and triumphant. We found that Jack only wagged his tail when he was pleased with himself but did not wag it for us.

In our bedroom is a full-length mirror on the wall, which is not apparent until one has walked into the room then turned to leave. Jack had a good look round but on turning to go out, caught sight of his reflection in the mirror. Stopping in his tracks, he looked a little taken aback yet quietly pleased and impressed, as if to say, "Oh, so that's what I look like." There was never any doubt in his mind that the image was himself. He didn't linger and went on to explore each room in turn. When he came to the bathroom, he knew he'd been in there before. A cheeky look came into his eye and he came out quickly.

It was decided that we had better teach Jack to descend the stairs, as it was plain to see that nothing would stop him from flying up them. I got into my position on the stairs below him and gave him great encouragement. He seemed more determined too, and put his trust in me, putting a front paw on the first stair down, then the next and so on. The only thing was, he left his back feet at the top and ended up a bit stretched out. I supported his chest whilst Mark got his back paws moving downwards, then I backed all the way down so Jack couldn't fall. This routine was carried on for a few weeks, as Jack would not descend unless I helped him. He would keep to the left on the way up and the same side, when he came down.

Teaching Jack to sit was quite easy, as he frequently sat, especially to defy us. I would take the opportunity to say, "SIT," when he was already sitting, then give him a dog biscuit or a small piece of cheese, which he would inspect, then take very gently from my fingers. He got the hang of it after the second time.

We tried Jack with various fruit and vegetables but it soon became evident that he was very particular in what passed his lips. Cooked broccoli florets were fine, as long as they were done to the correct consistency and did not include too much stalk. Jack didn't 'do' fruit. However, he loved fish, and if rice and peas were mixed with it, well, what the heck, it all tasted pretty fishy, so down it went. Fusilli pasta, especially with a homemade tomato sauce, was bolted in earnest. Low-fat cottage cheese, wholemeal bread (fresh or toasted), rice pudding, Shreddies, Shredded Wheat and porridge were all firm favourites, which we allowed Jack to share with us, or rather, what I could not fit in.

No food waste was put into the swing-bin in the kitchen; it all went in the bin outside or was taken for composting, so there would be no temptation for Jack to poke his pointy nose in and have a dabble about. All empty tins were thoroughly washed out and placed deep down in the kitchen bin. If it was rather full, empty tins would be put out of reach on the window sill behind the sink, until a new bin sack was in place. I did not want Jack to get a badly cut nose. Thankfully, he never showed a propensity for rooting in the bin.

Getting Jack to lie down, so I could clip his nails, was bit of a rigmarole. With Mark's help, we would lift him onto his right side, with me saying, "Lie down." Jack would push at me with his feet and get very silly because he wasn't quite sure what was going on and he didn't really know us very well. Mark made sure Jack didn't get up, whilst I clipped his nails using guillotine clippers. Before I'd made contact, Jack would yelp out, expecting pain. He had probably experienced his nails being cut into the quick previously and so thought I was going to do the same. He found that I didn't hurt him and was extremely pleased but felt a bit foolish afterwards for making such a fuss. Not that I blamed him; we all know the saying, "Once bitten, twice shy."

Jack's feeding time was kept at what he was used to, at midday and as near to his original diet. This was good quality chicken dog-meat with the consistency of paté, containing brown rice, peas and carrots. With this, I mixed a whole-wheat terrier-meal that was soaked first. His bowl would be up on the kitchen surface and when I was in the living room, I would hear strange clanging noises. Then I would find that Jack had jumped up at the surface and was busily scoffing his soaking biscuits. "GET DOWN," I shouted. And he would. "You're not supposed to eat that yet," I would tell him, he, licking his lips and looking sheepish. So, I put his bowl and biscuit-meal to soak on a high shelf, only to have him start to tell me that he preferred to eat earlier. And so he did, until it became his breakfast, which he was then satisfied with.

Occasionally, when Jack was eating his meal, the washing machine would be going through its cycles. As it was beside his feeding area, Jack would look through the porthole-window, in his earliest days, his head describing a circle as he followed the clothes in the drum, going round and round. Soon realising that it was nothing dangerous, he would only look up from his bowl if the machine rattled and shuddered, as it went into a spin. Mark and I, moving round the kitchen, also disturbed him from his food at first, as he wasn't used to people walking round him at feeding time. He soon got used to us being there, so much so that if anyone had asked him if we had been in the kitchen with him, at that time, he would have replied, "I don't know, I was busy eating."

The vacuum was seen as a roaring beast with a long, uncontrollable trunk, which swayed about bashing into things and was clearly, very frightening. Mark had to vacuum, as I was unable to and Jack would flee from whichever room was being cleaned. He would come to me for protection. I always told Mark to watch where the hose swung, so as not to frighten Jack anymore than he already was.

Noises on the television puzzled Jack, instead of the picture. Every time we watched Animal Hospital or Pet Rescue, and dogs could be heard barking or whining, Jack's ears were so upright to be almost crossing, his head cocked from one side to the other, so severely I thought his head was going to fall off. Out of his bed he would leap, rushing to look out of the window and when he couldn't see any sign of a dog outside, Jack then looked under tables, behind chairs and ran into other rooms to search further. He would be quite distressed and this in turn, distressed us. When I knew the programmes were about to start, I would turn the sound down on the television, so he wouldn't get so upset. Not only dog noises bothered Jack, but electronic sounds too. It really hurt me to see him nearly twisting his head right round, in order to work out what these strange noises were.

When walking Jack, we used a six and a half foot lead, of broad webbing, so as not to restrict him when he met other dogs. Not one of those extending leads, which I would not use with a greyhound because, if the dog suddenly shot off, (and they can do), it would be very difficult to stop the cord and a cord which hangs down, can quickly and easily become tangled around those slim legs, cutting the skin as the dog struggles to free itself. Jack also wore Jim's old collar; a broad leather one, specifically for a greyhound, bought in 1981 and still going strong.

When we met a dog, I didn't pull Jack towards me. I let him have the whole lead so he could do doggy things and to prevent any aggression. If another dog had started a fight, then Jack was free to react as he wished. He seemed very dominant and I thought he was aggressive. If he met another unneutered male, his tail curved high over his back, his neck arched, ears erect and nearly crossing, causing a frown, making him appear even more formidable. His eyes rolled and stared as he tiptoed around, growling. What a fearsome yet magnificent sight. Most males absolutely quaked and crept off, while Jack was unable to follow, as I held tightly onto the other end of his lead.

The time for Jack's teeth scaling had come. He spent the day at the vets until we could pick him up that evening. Having been with other dogs for the day, he was most upset to leave them. There was no recognition or wag of the tail. Still affected by the anaesthetic for the rest of the day, Jack was most unsettled, whining and staring blankly at us.

Jack was not typical of a greyhound and his distant, stubborn ways were beginning to stress me, often reducing me to tears. Although he wanted me with him at all times, Jack showed no affection whatsoever, even though Mark and myself showered him with love. Some of his characteristics I noted at the time were wilful, dominant, aggressive, stubborn, impatient and totally selfish. It got to the point where I couldn't stand life with Jack any longer and after discussions with Mark, I rang the trainer, who was not interested. In desperation, I contacted the RSPCA who were extremely reluctant to accept a greyhound, as nobody wants them. They could only take him if they had room. I had to ring them each week to try to book a space but was always unsuccessful. I tried other dog rescues all over the region and after much perseverance, one of them finally caved in under the pressure I was exerting. Phew.

Mark came home for lunch on that day, to be told by me, "I've found a place for Jack."

The Early Days

"I don't want him to go," said Mark, "I love him." When it came to the crunch, I couldn't do it. I loved Jack too and didn't want him passed from pillar to post, adding more to his current trauma. We decided to soldier on and hoped he would show signs of improvement some time in the future. It was now five weeks since bringing Jack home and he no longer barked at Mark, when he came home from work; so that was an improvement for a start.

Being very vocal and quick to complain, Jack was doing his best one morning, to climb into a cardboard box far too small for him that was on the lino in the dining room, containing carrots and potatoes in newspaper. I was reading at the time, sitting at the dining table. He soon caught my attention, though at first I could not make out what he was playing at. It looked as if Jack was trying to scrape the contents out onto the floor, while making small noises to himself. Suddenly it hit me what he was trying to tell me but I had to wait for Mark to come home, to be able to do anything about it. In the mean time I told Jack, "No, leave it," and so he did. I couldn't wait to tell Mark and as soon as he entered the house, I related the carrot and potato story, explaining that Jack was trying to tell me that he wanted a bed with sides. Mark disappeared for some time, to eventually re-appear with the bottom part of a large, old television box, made of triple-ply cardboard. I called Jack off his 'bed', picked up his blanket and sheepskin, while Mark put the cardboard bed down. I laid the blanket in the box, draping it over the sides to make it more comfortable and put the sheepskin in. Straight away Jack stepped in and lay down, letting a big sigh escape, with a very satisfied look on his face. I lent him a big old cushion to place in the step-through; otherwise he would spill out onto the floor when he stretched out.

A few days later, Jack was keeping me company in the dining room, lying on the lino which covered a concrete floor; so pretty hard and uncomfortable. He started to talk to me then got up to approach another box that we had on the floor. This one was even smaller; a wooden plant box full of carrots and newspaper. Jack pawed at the paper, trying to tear it using his teeth and making small whining noises. "Wait a minute," I said and went upstairs to unearth an old, single duvet from the airing cupboard. Luckily, it already had a cover on, so I folded it double and laid it in front of the dining room fireplace. Jack was on it before you could blink. It was better than that hard old floor and what's more, he could be comfortable whilst keeping an eye on Mummy!

Jack was with me in the living room one morning, when someone had walked past the window. Jack must have noticed them through the net curtain and jumping up, he rushed to the window, barking. I was impressed and praising him, as I did for anything he did which was good, decided to teach him to bark when someone knocked at the door. This meant that I did an awful lot of barking, every time anyone came to our door; sometimes Jack took the hint and joined in and sometimes he just let me bark. Eventually, he did turn out to be pretty good with his powerful voice.

Neither Mark nor I were too keen on the plastic muzzle that had been supplied for Jack. They are fine for racing, when they are worn for very short periods but I personally preferred the old wire ones, for a greyhound that will be wearing it for the duration of a walk. The plastic ones are boxed-in at the bottom, not allowing a dog that is hot and panting, to gasp in as much air as with a wire one, to enable it to cool down. Nor can they lap water when wearing a plastic muzzle. Wearing a wire muzzle, a greyhound can do all these things; it also appears more 'normal' to other dogs and can enjoy the many sniffs along the way.

Jack also needed a warm winter coat and a raincoat. Greyhounds need a warm coat for winter, as they don't have much fur, have virtually no body-fat and very thin skin. They have practically no undercoat, so get soaked to the skin in the rain, needing a rain mac for wet weather. So, off to the local dog track we went on a cold, wet night, to join all the dogs that were racing, as we entered the rear of the stadium. We thought Jack might get excited, want to go with the other dogs or become vocal but he didn't. We tried muzzles and coats on him until we were satisfied with the fit and ended up with a red waterproof, fleecy-lined walking-out coat, a red rain mac and a wire muzzle. We paid then ran back to the Land Rover to get out of the rain. To our amazement, Jack jumped in straight away. Was this to avoid the rain or was he glad we weren't leaving him at the racetrack?

During the week when Mark was at work, I would take Jack for a walk at various times of the day, having not got into a strict routine yet. We would walk across open fields where Jack would stop to stand whining quietly, staring into the distance. I didn't understand what was troubling him and it made me feel pretty bad. We would walk around the lake and down dusty tracks, past the church, along the road, exploring every inch. Some tracks we were unable to complete due to a cattle grid and a locked gate. When passing the opposite end of that track on a different walk, Jack would stop, stare up the track and pull to go that way, knowing that this must be the other end of the track which we never finished but wanting to satisfy himself that it was so.

If we came across a fallen tree or log, Jack would refuse to go on, staring and becoming quite worried, walking back and to on his lead, huffing through his lips. I would tell him it was all right, explain what the object was and say, "Come on, let's have a look," to encourage him. I would lead the way and Jack would follow cautiously whilst I continued to reassure him. On reaching the log or whatever had bothered him, I would touch it with my hand, look at Jack and say, "See, it's all right, it's just a log." Jack would then sniff it, find I was telling the truth, then with a look of, "Oh, it's only a log," cock his leg and wee on it, with a bit of scufting thrown in for good measure. I would always praise him for being brave and conquering his fears, which helped his confidence grow.

At that time there were a lot of sheep in the fields where we walked yet Jack never showed much interest, thank goodness, even when they ran en masse, across in front of us. There were also a lot of beef cattle and young but I never walked Jack through them in case they took umbrage at a greyhound. When mothers and young were on the other side of a fence one time, I approached with Jack, to see what they would do. It didn't surprise me when the mothers ganged up and came at us, along the fence-line. Jack was quite worried, as he knew he was the focus of their attention. I knew that would put him off investigating cattle; I wanted him to be wary of them.

As Jack wouldn't go to the toilet in the garden, I started taking him a very early morning, cold and frosty walk of about an hours duration. Usually the same route each day, across the fields, round the far side of the lake and back up the driveway. Jack seemed intent on getting to know every track on the estate and we both enjoyed these quiet walks, sometimes seeing the barn owl silently floating through the air on his quest for voles.

Mark would take Jack out last thing before bedtime and would come back with tales of where Jack had taken him. Mark would be taken to where Jack and I had walked. Jack would then set off investigating every nook and cranny, where I did not go with him, to discover whether certain paths linked with others. They would go 'off-road' too, Mark stumbling over fallen branches and tree roots and knocking his head on tree limbs above, due to being in total darkness. Although Mark was wearing a head-torch, it wasn't much help, as it kept fading, so he kept switching it off. Sometimes they went through a copse or down to a lodge, on the outskirts of the estate. Other times into a wooded area to inspect work that had been carried out, felling trees. All machinery needed to be sniffed at and usually a sprinkling of wee left on a suitable tyre. They would be gone an hour and I would be wondering what had happened to them. On their return, Mark would be muddy, tired and wanting to go to bed, whilst Jack would have liked to go further. Certainly not a typical greyhound, Jack seemed to have quite a lot of energy.

One November night, Mark and Jack were out on their walk, this time in the meadow, when Jack suddenly reared up at the end of his lead. Standing upright on his back legs, rather like a big kangaroo, he had heard or scented something. Mark could not see or hear anything. Without warning, Jack took off, dragging Mark hither and thither across the meadow, into the blackness. Poor Mark ran for all he was worth, not being able to see or stop. On reaching a fence, Jack stopped and whatever he had been hunting-down, must have carried on into the night. Mark was then able to regain control and was laughing and excited when he came home to tell his tale.

In these early days, on returning from a walk, Jack would not want to enter our garden. He would whine and pull to go back out again. Once in the garden, still on the lead, he reluctantly followed us to the back door, where he unwillingly entered the house. No amount of sweet-talking made any difference. I started to give him some dog biscuits when he came back from his walks, which did help to an extent but only time made the difference.

There were times when Jack would still refuse to enter the house after a walk, or even after he had just requested being let into the garden, from the house. Our lawn is raised, with six concrete steps down to a flat area, before the step up to the house. As I would stand holding the door open, calling, "Come on Jack," he would stand on the lawn looking, then sit down very slowly and decidedly, staring at me, his eye-level just above mine. Sometimes he would get up, just as decidedly, and stroll off in a contemptuous manner. He was defying me and controlling the situation. I soon realised this and would shut the door as soon as he sat down or stood looking. He would be left outside until he came to the door to ask to come in, which usually wasn't too long. I could tell by Jack's body language and the look on his face, that he didn't like being defeated. He had such an attitude and I hoped he would grow out of it.

In early November, we went for dinner at Mark's boss's, taking Jack with us. They had a three-legged Yorkshire terrier, Piper, who liked Mark and used to have a lurcher as a friend, so she accepted Jack, although kept him firmly in his place. While Jack was still very nervous of people at this time, it certainly didn't show on this night, as he accepted everyone as part of his family. While we sat around the dining table, Piper lay in the sitting room and would not allow Jack in there. He lay in the dining room or followed anyone into the kitchen or up the stairs, then had to be helped down. All in all, he thoroughly enjoyed himself.

The next morning, we were walking Jack in the field above the church, (the top field). Being empty of sheep or cattle, Mark wanted to let him off. I reluctantly agreed. Before we took his lead off, we walked the perimeter of the field, so that Jack knew where the barbed-wire fences were. I then fitted Jack's muzzle and let him go. To my surprise, he didn't go too far and behaved perfectly. This gave Mark and I hope.

The following morning, we thought we would try Jack in a section of the wood, which was fenced in, called the Deer Park. The cattle had been removed for the winter, so in we went. On went Jack's muzzle and off came his lead. He couldn't believe his luck, cantering off to look for those grey furry things, that he had seen when on the lead; they just looked so irresistible. As soon as he spotted one, Jack would be off like a shot, dodging and leaping any obstacles. The squirrel always disappeared up into the treetops, much to Jack's frustration. "There must be another, which I'll get," I could almost hear him saying to himself, as he rushed off to search the whole Deer Park. He would run the length and breadth, constantly out of our sight, with us trying to spot his red coat through the trees. My heart would be in my mouth as he dashed round, dreading that he may sustain an injury. After watching Pet Rescue and Animal Hospital on television, I knew how expensive a broken leg would be and decided to insure Jack.

In these early weeks, the Deer Park was the only place where we would let Jack off the lead, and then only when it was both Mark and I together. There was no way I could run after Jack if he misbehaved and ran off. It was usually very early in the morning at the weekend, when we hardly saw a soul, that we roamed the Deer Park.

One beautiful sunny morning, we tramped back and to, whilst Jack flew round, ears erect, eyes alert, keen to catch sight of any movement, tail high and panting into the frosty air. He ran towards the donkey paddock, at one corner of the 'Park. "Jack," we called. "Can he get out over there?" I said to Mark. "I don't think so," he replied, just as Jack appeared from the other side of the donkey's stable. "He's in the donkey paddock," I shouted. We both ran forward. The donkeys were both standing with their backs to a corner and Jack, relieved to see company, ran towards them. "Heehaw, heehaw, heehaw," shouted the donkeys. Jack skidded to a halt, turned tail and dashed off in the direction he had come. Mark and I fell about laughing then Mark went to rescue Jack, who was pleased with himself for having survived such an ordeal but looking a bit foolish.

On another early morning foray, the low sun slanted through the leafless trees. Jack careered round as usual, looking for and chasing any squirrels that happened to be on the ground. We were about a hundred yards away and spotted him flying along towards the donkey paddock, into the sun's rays. My stomach turned over as I realised he couldn't see the barbed wire. We were so far away, all I could see was Jack bounce and yelp out then stand still. Mark and I ran as fast as we could, "Stand still, stand still," I shouted as Jack started to move. My heart pounded and I felt weak as we reached him, his coat hanging around his neck and his wire muzzle bent. We both checked his body; his shoulders, thighs, sides, legs, chest, neck all fine. I straightened his coat and found tears in the fabric on one shoulder and the opposite thigh area. The coat had saved Jack from serious injury. His muzzle had also saved him from too much contact with the wire but his left ear had been torn. The blood flowed freely onto his collar and coat, matting the hair as it congealed. I couldn't see how bad the injury was until we got home and I cleaned the blood off his fur. Thank goodness it was only a small cut; what a huge relief for all of us. It must have felt numb at first because Jack didn't seem to mind me tending to it but later on, if anyone stroked him and touched that ear, he would yelp out. Once healed, he was back to normal, not minding his ears being stroked.

I had been thinking for some time that Jack couldn't make do with a cardboard bed for too long, as it would fall to pieces. He needed a wicker basket, like Jim used to have yet we never saw any in the pet shops. Mark knew a chap, Adrian, who did wicker work, so we thought we would ask him to make one for Jack. It took quite a few phone calls to track Adrian down and once I'd spoken to him, he sounded like a really nice man. He told me to decide what size I wanted, then we could pay a visit to his workshop, to look at different styles. I waited until Jack was lying in his cardboard bed, then out came the tape measure. It was impossible to remember what size Jim's bed was, so I tried to remember what he looked like in his bed; how much room he had. The basket for Jack had to be circular and after many minutes of measuring, tutting and re-measuring, I decided on forty-one inches inside diameter. I phoned Adrian, to see if that was o.k. "That's huge!" he exclaimed, "Are you sure?" "Yes," I replied, "I've measured and that looks right to me."

We arranged a visit to his house, one dark, windy night, taking Jack along too, as we didn't like to leave him unnecessarily. We were welcomed into a small cottage in the middle of nowhere and Jack, being pleased to be included, had to have a good look at everything. After I had explained to Adrian, the design of one foot-high sides with a step-through and given him a drawing, Mark, who had Jack on the lead, became aware that Jack had stiffened and was concentrating on a fish tank, on the floor. "Oh, that's my little boy's hamster," said Adrian. "Hang on to Jack," I told Mark, as the hamster stood up at the front of the tank, to look at Jack. Poor Jack was trembling in anticipation, ready to pounce. It really wasn't fair to keep him there, so we took him to the other side of the room, out of temptations way. "I don't know when I'll be able to make your basket, as I've got a lot on at the moment," Adrian said. "That's o.k." I replied, "Whenever you can. Just give me a ring." And we left it at that.

Early December, one afternoon, I heard our window cleaner, Leigh, clanging his ladders about next door. "This should be interesting," I thought, wondering what Jack would do once Leigh reached our house. Sitting in the dining room, with Jack lying on his duvet, I waited. Suddenly, crash bang, went the ladders against the side of the house. Jack jumped up, rushing to the window, as Leigh ascended his ladder. "Woof," I barked and Jack joined in quickly, barking all the while that Leigh worked. I pulled the net curtain back so Leigh could see Jack and said, "See you round the other side." When Leigh came to do the back windows, I let him meet Jack, who was a bit unsure but said hello anyway. Leigh thought Jack was lovely, being a dog-lover himself and said he looked forward to getting to know Jack.

Jack's confidence had grown considerably, which showed itself when he cocked his leg very high, to do a wee, tail also held high, then he would scrape furiously at the ground; grass, soil and sticks being hurled ten to twenty feet behind him. Jack took great delight in this and if I was behind him, holding his lead, he would either fill my Wellingtons with debris or occasionally thwack his foot into me, then look round as if to say, "I do beg your pardon," would turn back and carry on the walk.

By this time, we had developed a routine of the main walk being early afternoon, Jack settling into this and starting to enjoy himself. Part of the walk would be along the road and across fields. We also started to explore the Great Wood more. Small circular routes were favourite at first, as I did not wish to get lost. On one of these incursions, we bumped into the foreman of the wood yard, carrying out some clearance work, who had brought his dog, Satan, along to save leaving him at home. I asked if Jack could say hello to Satan, as I wanted him to meet as many dogs as possible. Martin, the foreman, agreed. Jack wagged his tail and whined. Satan, a small Manchester terrier, reared up and put his front paws against Jack's chest, growling, but nothing more. Not wanting to push things too far, I slowly drew Jack away and we carried on our walk.

Jack, being extremely inquisitive, soon got bored with this small circuit and forced me to try a larger route. He was never satisfied, so over a further few weeks, we gradually built up our knowledge of every twist and turn of the whole wood. When we followed a new path, to emerge onto a familiar track, Jack would recognise the old track straight away, whilst I had to stand and get my bearings first. He would look at me as if he thought I was wasting time and must have thought his human, very slow and stupid.

We started to meet the regular dog-walkers and there were quite a few, which pleased Jack no end. A large yellow Labrador and wire-haired fox terrier came towards us, one afternoon, so I stopped and allowed Jack the whole of his lead. All dogs bristled and Jack's lead vibrated as he growled. I was hoping everything would be all right. The lady and man, accompanying the dogs, said, "Hello," and walked on calling their names, "Jaffa," "Come on Taxa," and the dogs slowly moved off. In one way, I wished Jack didn't seem so on-the-defensive and in another, I was glad he wasn't frightened of other dogs.

We also met two retired ladies with about five small dogs; terriers and King Charles spaniels. Some used to bark at Jack, so he kept out of their way and the rest ran to say hello, fawning and smiling around his feet. Jack wagged his tail and sniffed delicately at them through his muzzle. Even when they darted around, Jack never showed any propensity to go after them. This pleased me because there would be less likelihood of him chasing a small dog when off the lead.

One Sunday evening, we decided to try Jack off the lead in the Great Wood. As far as he was concerned, he was out to hunt and once off the lead, he could do as he liked. His pace was a fast trot, which made keeping up with him extremely difficult. Then Jack spotted his first squirrel of the walk, galloped off and disappeared. Being on a particularly muddy and slippery track, we were prevented from hurrying after him. "Jack, Jack," we shouted to no avail, running once we reached firmer ground. Suddenly, Jack ran up from behind then promptly dived into the brambles at the base of a tree, eyes skyward in the hope of spotting the squirrel that had dashed up there. We persuaded him to come along, with lots of cuddles. This pattern was repeated around the wood.

On reaching a track that ran above and parallel to a road, Jack was intent on following dog-walker's tracks through the bracken, down to the road. It wasn't a busy road but it was a road and we didn't want Jack down there. Off he would trot in the most determined fashion and no amount of calling would have any effect. His ears never even flicked, to show that he could hear us. I would send Mark after him, as my back wouldn't stand all this. Mark would be running along behind, as Jack trotted along the road. Where he thought he was going, I don't know. I was beginning to think that he was deaf. Mark really had to shout loudly and sternly, before Jack would stop and look at Mark with some surprise. Jack would be led back, with Mark firmly holding his collar, wagging his tail in a sheepish yet innocent way. I would snap his lead on and explain that it was naughty to run off; he should stay with us. We would let Jack off again and for about ten minutes, he would stay in our vicinity until we turned onto a sidetrack and called him. Jack would carry on for some way, on the original track, before we could get him to come our way. By this time, I was convinced Jack was deaf or just plain stubborn. There was no way I was going to let him off, when on my own. So, walks with Mummy were always on the lead.

The more freedom Jack had off the lead, the more he calmed down, apart from when he met Rowan, a nine month old yellow Labrador male, in the Deer Park. Rowan was owned by Mary, our churchwarden, who looked after the donkeys, feeding and watering them twice daily and who tirelessly helped many people. Rowan, who was exceedingly boisterous, encouraged Jack to chase him, then quickly regretted it, as Jack was on him in seconds, bowling him over in the mud and pinning him down. Then Jack would stand and wait for Rowan to go again. Rowan, being so young, always thought, this time he could out-manoeuvre Jack but he was always wrong, as there was just no escape from this growling, black whirlwind. Jack's growling wasn't aggressive, as he never curled his lip back to show his canines; it was pure excitement, (it's a greyhound thing) and Labradors who ran away, excited him. Jack always wore his muzzle off the lead, so no damage could come of this excitement. Mary's patience and understanding was much appreciated, as Jack needed to get this out of his system and we all hoped they would become good friends.

Occasionally on a Sunday, we would have a little lie-in but not for too long, as Jack didn't approve at all. We would go for a woodland walk before breakfast and quite often bumped into a lady and her daughter, who had two young Labrador bitches, Honey, a yellow and Lottie, a black one. Jack thought they were very exciting, especially Lottie, whom he chased and mercilessly knocked about. She was terrified, as she could not shake off her persistent pursuer. Mark and I would shout Jack's name and try our best to catch him, quite unsuccessfully. I felt so ashamed of Jack's behaviour. I assumed the ladies must think us all awful. Poor Lottie suffered this rough treatment most Sundays, for some weeks to come.

If a greyhound has had a racing career, this is how it can act at first; be a complete hooligan. This doesn't mean that they should be kept on the lead all the time; they do grow out of it. Everything does become so old-hat and they become ever so refined, looking at other dogs that run madly about and jump on them, as if to say, "Do you mind not being so vulgar." However, Jack wasn't quite at this stage yet.

A couple of weeks prior to Christmas, we were settled eating our tea, which was a big pasta-bowl each of rice, peas, salmon and tuna fish, Jack lying in his bed, when a knock at the front door sounded. Jack leapt up barking, getting in our way, as we both went to the door. High-pitched voices sounded as the village children started their carol. We opened the door and the singing tailed-off, young faces staring and Mary smiling at us in our dressing gowns, all of them looking slightly embarrassed, when all they had done was to interrupt our meal. "Carry on," said Mark. Up piped the voices. I handed over some money and as if by magic, they vanished to our next-door neighbours, Gill and Henry, to irresistible, edible delights. Maybe I didn't give them enough money or maybe it was the food next door!

We closed the door and realised that Jack wasn't with us. Into the living room we rushed, to see him scoffing what was left of Mark's tea, rice scattered around him in his haste. "Oi," shouted Mark, "Leave it." Jack knew he'd done something wrong and went to lie in his bed. "He's eaten all my tea," complained Mark. "Well, you'd eaten most of it. There's nothing you can do about it now," I replied. Jack obviously thought we'd finished and had helped himself. We didn't give him any leftovers that night.

It wasn't the fish, rice and peas that made Jack so flatulent but they may have helped. I remarked to Mark, "I don't know about Scrumpy Jack, I think we should call him Trumpy Jack," and it stuck. All greyhounds are extremely flatulent, I think more so than other dogs. It's a natural thing, so it never bothered us. Most of his wind was silent but some made a hissing noise, or even a raspberry sound, which quite concerned Jack. His ears would flick up and he would stretch to sniff his bottom, to make sure it was all right. He was quite good at burping too, usually in one of our faces, as we stroked him after a meal.

Just before Christmas, we travelled up to my Mum's near Manchester; a journey of around two hundred miles. Jack's first long-haul trip. All our bags and boxes were strapped onto the seat-benches in the back of the Land Rover, to leave the floor space clear for Jack. He already had a sheepskin in there and on top of this, we piled his cardboard bed, complete with blankets and sheepskin; his big cushion, which we put between the bed and the rear door and to top things off, his doubled-up duvet. He was going up in the world, literally.

With the weather forecast being for snow from the west, we dubiously set off, hoping that it would not be as bad as predicted yet feeling more secure in the Land Rover than we would have done in a car. We also carried hot drinks, food for ourselves and for Jack; all wore warm clothing and had two duvets with us, (the second being for Mark and I to use at my Mum's). The only snow we encountered was between Kings Lynn and Grantham, which covered the roads rapidly and effortlessly. It was headlights and slow progress, as the wind drove the snowflakes across our windscreen. Cars swerved from side to side as they crawled along, a few had been abandoned on the verges, one bonnet-first in a ditch. Once through Grantham, the roads were clear, enabling us to make good time.

Although Jack whined at first, he had to resign himself to the fact that this was a long journey and finally dozed, without laying his head down. Near Derby, we all stretched our legs and had a drink and a bite to eat, before we continued our travel.

On arrival at my Mum's, Jack was glad to get out of the vehicle and happy to enter another person's house, to have a good nosey. I held Jack on the lead, until Mark had brought everything in; I didn't want him slipping out into the street and setting off to explore. This done, I told my Mum, "We're going shopping, we'll leave Jack with you." "No. I'm not being left with him," Mum protested. "He'll be all right, we won't be long," I said as we went out and closed the front door.

After visiting the local supermarkets, for our provisions, we returned to be greeted by, "Never again, never again. You're never leaving him with me again." "O.k. o.k." I said, "Why, what's he done?" "He cried the whole time you were out," she raged. Oh dear. We thought he might. It wasn't surprising really; he probably believed we had left him and were not coming back. "He stole some butter and he jumped on the settee," she said, "To look out of the window." He never jumped on the furniture in our house and never showed any interest in doing so. He must have done this in desperation, looking for us. When my Mum told Jack to get off, he had sat down and looked at her, refusing to budge. She said Jack was defying her. And he was. "Jim was never like that," said my Mum. "No he wasn't," I thought. Jim was very laid back. That was the last thing that Jack was. Jack soon calmed down, after telling us off for leaving him and after we'd had something to eat, we took him for a walk.

There being no door which could shut off the stairs, left Jack free to run up and down, as and when he pleased. By this time, he had well and truly mastered the art of ascending and descending the stairs, so he took full advantage of this opportunity. As bedtime approached, we discussed what to do with Jack; should he sleep downstairs? But then we knew he would pop straight up again, to look for us. My Mum liked to sleep with her bedroom door open and was worried that Jack would go in at night, (yes he would), or that he would lie on the landing and she would trip over him, if she got up to go to the toilet. It ended up with Jack's bed in our room and one overjoyed greyhound. Being quite chilly, I covered Jack with a travel rug and we all slept peacefully. Until five a.m., that is, when Jack got up, shook himself, his ears flapping loudly on the sides of his head. Whining, he came over to look at me. He didn't have far to look, as Mark and I were lying on a mattress, on the floor. I pretended to be asleep. Jack put himself to bed. Shortly, up he got again and came over to me, crying. I reached out my hand to him. Knowing then that I was awake, he got quite agitated, crying a little louder and stretching; first his shoulders and front legs, then his back legs, obviously trying to tell me something. I got up. He ran to the bedroom door. On my opening it, down the stairs Jack ran and straight to the back door. Down I stumbled and let him out into the garden, where he did a poo straight away, then ran back in, up the stairs and into his bed. After locking up, I followed him and covered him with his rug before snuggling down myself, to finish my sleep. On other nights, Jack would wake me to tell me that he was cold, so that I could cover him over with his rug again.

We didn't really need an alarm clock with Jack, because he was guaranteed to be tuning up, if we weren't at six a.m. sharp. The next morning, Jack climbed onto our mattress and lay against me. "Get off," I said quite loudly and tried to push him off. He completely ignored me. As I was pinned down, Mark had to get up and get hold of Jack's collar, to make him get off. He had to be told quite a few times, quite sternly, not to get onto the mattress over the next few days and eventually he did abandon the idea.

Before breakfast, we walked on the local playing field, across the railway, not letting Jack off, as there were far too many tempting paths that led to busy roads and we didn't trust him enough in this situation, yet. He still found it quite enjoyable, though this was deemed a little boring.

My Mum scattered peanuts on the lawn for 'her' grey squirrel, which visited daily. After breakfast, along came Squirrel down the garden. Jack saw him through the dining room window, as we had told him to, "Look out of the window." He couldn't believe it. One of those familiar grey, furry things that he chased in the woods. Jack's body trembled and his eyes intently pierced the squirrel, as Mark held Jack's collar. I thought it probably best to let Jack out to give chase, so that he would know that the way out was through the back door and not through the window. Mark took him to the back door. I knelt on the settee, looking out of the window.

Squirrel wandered off up the garden. Good. This would lessen Jack's chances. On hearing the back door opening, Squirrel, thinking it was my Mum, came back towards the house. Oh no! I called out but Mark couldn't hear me. The next second, Jack appeared round the corner of the washhouse. Squirrel, hair stood on end, tail stuck up into the air like a bottlebrush, went supersonic and shot up the garden, with Jack two inches off his tail all the way. For a moment, any concerns left me and I burst out laughing. I'd never seen anything like it in my life before. It was certainly worthy of a Tom and Jerry cartoon and I clung onto the settee, in fits, tears running down my face. Squirrel swarmed up the fence, into next-door's garden and Jack nearly went with him, over the six-foot barrier. Not that he thought he could jump it; he was just so close to catching Squirrel, so worked up and also, so inexperienced in when it was best to stop. Unfortunately, he must have landed on a pile of bricks but never felt any discomfort due to being fuelled with adrenalin. We were not aware of any injuries at the time, apart from a cut nail bed, which always requires immediate attention, being bathed with Listerine (original) and having Negasunt wound powder applied every time Jack went outside, until it was fully healed. If neglected, infection can set in rapidly and the toe swell to enormous proportions.

The same day, we visited my old vet, to ask why the tip of one of Jack's ears was lumpy and the hair falling out. The vet spotted injuries but didn't mention them, being used to me knowing every scratch on my dog and presuming that we were aware of them. We weighed Jack in at 28.20kg and were given two lots of drops for his ears; one for wax and one for the ear tips.

Later that day, when Jack was roly-polying, we saw cuts and bruises in his groin and on his rib area. I applied Listerine to the cuts and fervently hoped there had been no internal damage. I walked up the garden to see what could have caused the harm and came to the conclusion, it must have been the pile of bricks. It was watching Jack chase the squirrel that made me realise, he didn't view it as 'fun', as with Jim, when he used to chase cats out of the garden, but he was deadly serious. When Squirrel came down the garden, another day, I told Mark that on no account was Jack to be alerted to the fact; it was far too dangerous.

Mark and I went to two parties, that holiday. Because my Mum would not allow Jack to be left with her, we had to take him and leave him in the Land Rover. We made him as comfortable as possible, with his duvet, his coat on and his travel rug, yet I constantly worried about him and felt guilty that he would be anxious and fretful. We never went away at Christmas again.

Late December, we returned home and it was nice to get back to normal and to the woods. Three days later, we invited Leigh, the window cleaner and Richard, a good friend of ours, for a meal. Although, on their arrival,

Jack barked and wagged his tail at the same time, he soon settled down and enjoyed having company, especially as there was food involved. He was very well behaved, having learnt a considerable amount of manners, albeit, they still needed some refinement. He had discovered that if he didn't whine with impatience but exercised some quiet restraint, he would be rewarded by some tit-bits, at the end of the meal. Every time I walked into the kitchen, Jack danced attendance, eyes beaming in eager anticipation. "Sit," I said and his bottom was on the floor before the words were barely out of my mouth. "Just give me the food," I could almost hear him saying. The evening was culminated by sipping hot Norfolk punch; sitting round a toasty, log fire, chatting about everything and nothing, whilst Jack lay in his bed, asleep.

CHAPTER 3

Various Meetings and The Black Controller

It was the Millennium and it didn't really feel any different. We were on our usual trip around the Deer Park, Jack charging madly about every time he spotted a squirrel. One minute he was behind us, the next, on our right or left; we just couldn't keep up. Suddenly, there was Jack flying along from the left, way ahead of us. His chosen squirrel, belting towards a large tree, which was surrounded by a large pile of logs and brambles. The squirrel skimmed over these and up the trunk. Jack took a flying leap and disappeared from view, behind the tree buttress.

Both of us expected to see him emerge from the other side. Nothing. Just silence. "Where is he?" we both said, looking at each other, then breaking into a run. On reaching the other side of the tree, there was Jack, chest-deep in brambles and jumbled logs, looking slightly silly. How he had landed, is anybody's guess. How he had ended up facing the way he had jumped in, is an even bigger mystery. He made an attempt to get to us, from his prison, whereupon we told him to, "Stand still." Mark climbed in to hoist Jack carefully up in his arms. I climbed in, to steady and guide Mark and we both stumbled and tripped our way to safe ground, Jack happily safe in his saviours grasp.

At the end of a Saturday evening walk, with Jack on the lead, we met a cousin of Mark's, with her two lively dogs; a chocolate Labrador and a bearded collie, who both raced round Jack, which frustrated him no end. As he wasn't muzzled, we did not let him off.

The next morning, as we followed Jack around the Deer Park on his squirrel foray, we found ourselves opposite the place where we met the two dogs, the previous night. Jack, determined to see if they were still about, squeezed under the barbed wire – luckily he was wearing his coat – to trot up and down, sniffing the ground and looking in every direction. Mark and I thought Jack would be off down the nearest track but he surprised us by staying in the one area. Eventually, as he couldn't persuade us to follow him, he came back into the Deer Park, through the gate we held open for him; to much praise, of course.

On the first Friday in January, Adrian called to say Jack's basket was ready and it was arranged for Mark to pick it up the following Tuesday.

Tuesday came. Mark set off to be at Adrian's for 5.30p.m. while I stayed at home with Jack. Some time later, Mark returned and as he carried the basket into the living room, where I sat, my mouth dropped open. It was huge. "It only just fitted into the Land Rover," said Mark. I was speechless. Adrian had been right. Well I couldn't do much about it now. I got Jack to reluctantly vacate his cardboard bed. Mark put the basket down in its place and I positioned the blanket. Oh dear, I needed another blanket as well. The sheepskin looked rather small in the big bed and I couldn't take the borrowed cushion away; it did help fill up the space, to some extent. We indicated to Jack that he could climb in, which he did, only to curl up very small, at the back, looking totally disgruntled as Mark left the room with his cardboard bed.

Jack didn't speak to Mark for two days. The next Saturday, we managed to find two cushions, in a charity shop, to help bulk out the bed. By this time, Jack had accepted his 'big bed', as it became known and luxuriated in being able to stretch out completely, head on cushions, sinking into his sheepskin. This was his safe haven, especially from the vacuum.

By the middle of February, another lot of dog food needed to be ordered. I ordered in bulk and bought sacks of biscuit meal, boxes of dog biscuits and usually around eight trays of tins, each tray containing twelve tins.

Always delivered on a Friday, this particular day, the driver arrived at our door carrying the eight trays, like a swaying tower block. Jack always answered the door with me; he just had to be included in everything – didn't want to miss a trick. Well, the inevitable happened, as Simon stepped over the threshold. Down tumbled the trays, crashing to the floor. Jack flew. Through the dining room, through the kitchen and into the living room. I ran after him to tell him it was all right. He was quite good at facing up to his fears and also trusted me, so came round to the dining room, to see Simon and to lie down while I paid.

We waved goodbye then Jack had to inspect the tins, sacks and boxes, delicately sniffing, eyes shining, tail wagging, knowing it was all his. Later, when Mark came home, in the evening and carried Jack's food upstairs, Jack kept well out of the way, just in case.

A few days later and gorgeous weather. We'd all had our before-breakfast-walk in the Deer Park, finished all our weekend tasks, had a bite to eat for lunch and came to a decision to drive to Holkham beach.

It was time to try Jack off the lead somewhere different from the usual. Of course, he had to be lifted into the Land Rover and was quite upset at being cooped up, instead of walking straight from the house.

On arrival at Holkham, Jack was happy to leap out of the vehicle and eager to explore. Along a sandy path, we entered the pinewoods, where I muzzled Jack and let him off the lead. Trotting quickly, it looked as though Jack was going to disappear, with no regard for us. Mark ran after him while we both called, "Jack, wait." There he was, around the next corner, waiting. He kept within our sight and did as he was told until he found a narrow track, in a dip and was nowhere to be seen by the time we reached it.

"Jack, Jack," we called and kept calling, when suddenly we spotted him, in his red coat, running through the trees, making his way to us in a very round about way, nearly slipping in his haste. Praising him for returning, we then walked on or rather, marched on, quick time.

On spotting a dog through the trees, surprisingly Jack stayed with us when I told him, "No. Stay here," instead of racing off to see it. He also had a friendly encounter with a Labrador, before we continued on our way. We came to a track on the edge of the wood, bordered by a large hedge in places, with open fields beyond. Jack trotted ahead, enjoying the many scents, ignoring small sidetracks and the open fields. So far, so good.

As we approached a junction, two horses and riders crossed ahead. Jack stopped and stared. Although we told him to wait, I think he had no intention of proceeding at all. He resumed his sniffing, as if to say, "I'll pretend there's a really good smell here, to give Mummy and Daddy time to catch up, in case I need protection. I don't know what they were but they were pretty big."

We took the opportunity of gaining the corner before him, just in case any more horses were about. Jack having caught us up, we turned onto the boardwalk and made our way towards the beach, only to bump into a red setter male, who looked as if he had something he wanted to say. Jack met him face-to-face, making the other dog quickly back down, even though Jack was smaller. He followed it and pushed it about a bit – he liked to barge, using his strong shoulders. I stepped in, grasping his coat hood, pulling him away. The owners were a young couple, with a little girl. She asked if Jack was going to bite. "Oh no," I answered confidently then realised I didn't really know what his intentions were. Not that he could have bitten anyway; he was wearing his muzzle. The only other dogs Jack met before we reached the beach were two King Charles spaniels whom Jack sniffed, good-naturedly for a brief second, then realising that we were ahead of him, quickly overtook us.

Trotting down the narrow, sandy path between two banks, brought Jack quite suddenly onto the huge expanse of Holkham beach. Stopping, looking left and right, he made a small sound of exclamation, just like a person would. We passed Jack as he stood in utter amazement, before he joined us, trotting by, knocking our legs with his muzzle, as he tried to rub it off.

Whilst Mark and I ploughed through a slimy, wet patch of sand, Jack trotted round the perimeter, meeting us at the other side. He was being such a good boy; we were so pleased. Oh no. Spoke too soon. On the horizon was a group of people with three dogs, the smallest walking a few feet ahead. This was worth investigation and an excuse for a good burn-up, so off Jack galloped, taking watery channels in his stride. There was just no point in calling him. Greyhounds have superior eyesight and can cover the ground in seconds and if they spot something they want to examine in the distance, off they jolly well go. This is usually in the early months of your relationship – they do develop the 'been there, done that' attitude and just can't be bothered later on.

Jack's brakes were applied prior to reaching the small dog and he broke into a trot. From our distant position, the encounter looked amicable enough, with Jack soon turning his attention to the owners and their two further dogs. He, very happily, trotted along with this group, as we continued to close the gap. We called him a few times. He looked over twice then cantered towards us a short way, stopping some distance ahead on our intended route and waited. Hmmm. Jack certainly did not like to backtrack. On reaching him, he greeted us, bashing our legs with his muzzle and poking his nose through our legs from behind. "Mind my testicles," exclaimed Mark in mock indignation.

Jack stayed with us a little while until a young dog, on a lead, with a couple, was noticed. Off he ran again. Being nearer this time, we followed. The dog was a bouncing, German shorthaired pointer puppy; just the sort of creature to excite Jack to chase. I grabbed his coat hood. The couple were friendly and chatty yet clearly had the wrong impression of ex-racing greyhounds, commenting that we were lucky that Jack was not a killer. We parted, still holding Jack, releasing him after a short distance and telling him, "This way." For a few seconds, he did as he was bid but just could not resist running back to the bouncing puppy, still excited by the prospect of a game – Jack style and one which he would win, naturally. Once again, we retrieved him with apologies, keeping a firm hold until well away.

In front of us was a group of young men with a sand-buggy and three young men trying to keep their feet on the ground, while flying a buggy parachute. Jack was intrigued. What on earth was going on? He had to have a look. We were concerned that he kept away, as the large parachute regularly crashed onto the sand with a loud and very heavy thud. Running towards the sea, we called Jack and sure enough, he raced after us, continuing to run in large curves. One of these curves took him back to the parachute-boys, so we walked off along the beach, calling him. He arrived just as we reached a small terrier that was digging a hole in the sand. Of course, Jack had to poke his nose in, only to be told by a snarl, lunge and snap, that he wasn't wanted. He took the hint and trotted off with us.

This beach is big, with a feeling of space. Although never appearing crowded, it still gets busy with people and dogs, leaving Jack spoilt for choice. He went bothering a Bichon frisé, which launched itself at his muzzle. Jack jumped back, hung around for a while then giving up, came to our calls. A couple approaching with two Labradors, rushed to put them on their leads as soon as they saw Jack. One evaded capture, coming forward to say a quick hello before being dragged off unceremoniously, by its owner, who never uttered a word, annoyed because his dog had not stayed by his side.

I put Jack on the lead, as he had had plenty of freedom and we were nearing the end of the beach and our exit. We made our weary way back to the Land Rover, Jack actually being glad to get in and lie down. I think it is safe to say that he enjoyed his excursion.

Jack was still kept on the lead when I took him out on my own. We enjoyed our walks, starting to recognise the local dog-walkers and getting to know them. The wire-haired fox terrier, Jaffa, whom we met earlier, was one and was owned by Daisy. Although Jaffa had been neutered, you wouldn't have known and sniffing his bottom was a definite no, no. Jack didn't know this, making the simple mistake one fine day, of poking his nose under Jaffa's tail. Like lightening, Jaffa turned on him. Lots of growling and snarling between them, then Jack pulled back. He didn't want a fight. Daisy dragged Jaffa away, as Jack had backed into the undergrowth by the barbed wire fence. A tuft of Jaffa's hair hung from Jack's mouth. He stood in the path, tilting his head from side to side, as he listened to Daisy giving Jaffa a good dressing down. "I'm so sorry Ann," said Daisy, "He always swears at dogs who sniff his bottom." "It's all right," I answered, "They didn't bite each other. It was all noise. I don't think Jack will sniff his bottom again."

Before this incident, Jack and Jaffa had become good friends, feeling free and easy in each other's company. The next time they met, they both seemed awkward, embarrassed and passing like ships in the night, ignored each other.

Another dog we bumped into a lot, was Taxa the Labrador male, owned by Bob. Taxa was a big, kindly soul – a gentle giant but he wasn't neutered, so Jack took great delight in pushing him to the limits. Jack would strut round Taxa, knocking into him, growling and generally being a complete pain. Taxa was a bit taken aback at first. However, he soon realised that Jack didn't mean any real harm, so got used to growling at this absolute nuisance. Not that it put Jack off. I used to apologise to Bob and tell him that Jack would calm down eventually, hoping that it would be sooner rather than later.

Jack and I had just emerged from the Deer Park, one day, onto a grassy ride, when Jack espied Martin, the foreman of the wood yard, with his Land Rover, further up the ride. Jack had to stare, as he wanted to know what was happening, and refused to move. Satan appeared, who was usually tied up although, not on this occasion. Barking, Satan ran down towards us. I let Jack have the whole of his lead, not being sure quite what was going to happen. As Satan closed in, Jack looked on in disbelief at the small form hurtling for him. In seconds, Satan came straight for Jack but leapt back in shock as Jack snapped with such speed and accuracy, just catching Satan's nose and drawing blood, that Satan stood back, taking stock of the situation – most big dogs were nowhere near as quick as this one. Jack stood stiffly, every muscle standing out, an indignant look on his face. Satan very carefully backed off, making sure he was some distance away before turning to run back to Martin.

Near the end of February, we drove up to visit my Mum and were quite shocked to find she had not been out for a few days, due to chest pains. She insisted it was a chest infection. I wasn't having that and rang for the doctor. Angina was diagnosed, with two lots of tablets prescribed. Mum didn't want to take any pills, still insisting it wasn't her heart. After coming for a walk with us, suffering chest pains and popping a pill under her tongue, she found her symptoms relieved. She was overjoyed. We felt a whole lot better too. Things were back to normal.

Jack would sleep upstairs with us at night, in his old cardboard bed, which we kept as his holiday bed and around seven a.m. as soon as we opened the bedroom door, he would rush downstairs to the kitchen, where my Mum was cutting her bread. He sat to beg for tit-bits and Mum was very impressed with how gently Jack accepted the offerings. This happened every morning.

After breakfast, we would all go for a wander to the field over the railway and even let Jack off. It was up to Mark to chase him, if necessary. Only once did Jack scamper down a path, onto a small housing estate where Mark found him standing gazing round and returned him to the field.

On our return to the house, a cup of tea and toasted teacake were the order of the day. Mum had put her plate containing two pieces of teacake, onto a small side-table, then left the dining room. Mark and I were in the kitchen. On settling ourselves in the dining room, Mark noticed that there was only one piece of teacake on Mum's plate. I scrutinized the plate. Not a crumb visible; the single piece perfect and undisturbed. "Did she have two?" I asked Mark. "I think so," he replied. "Jack must have had it," I said. The little monkey! Those small, nibbly front teeth were excellent for delicate work. He wasn't greedy though, as he had left the other half for Mum. When she entered the room, she confirmed that there were indeed two pieces originally but didn't begrudge Jack taking his share first. We didn't say anything to Jack about it, as he lay serenely on the carpet, head on paws, looking totally unaware of the disappearance of a piece of teacake.

The rest of the week went well, Jack accompanying us into town, visiting my cousin Carol for a meal and being much admired by all. Carol thought him, 'a little treasure.' Her friends being quite astounded by his likeness to Anubis. Jack's manners improved all the time, although he still approached dining tables, sniffing the aromas and pointing at things he thought smelt interesting and being totally overjoyed when we saved him small delicacies, at the end of the meal.

By Friday morning, Mum was complaining that one lot of her tablets made her arms and legs feel very uncomfortable. I phoned the doctor and arranged for someone to visit her that day. Jack had just come in from the garden and was standing in the washhouse. As I looked at him, my eyes were drawn to a dark spot on the floor, underneath him. It turned out to be blood dripping from his penis. Oh great. I presumed it was a bladder

26

infection, due to him licking bitches urine from grass. As we were travelling home that day, there wasn't much I could do at that moment.

Everything packed in the Land Rover, including ourselves, we waved goodbye to Mum, who was herself waving madly and blowing kisses from an upstairs window. This was very unusual for her and I felt quite strange, not wanting to leave; yet I knew I must. Driving off, we discussed Mum, coming to the conclusion that she was very lonely since Dad had died, the year before.

Once home, we took Jack to the vet. A sample of urine was clear, so his prostate was checked, which Jack thoroughly disapproved of, deafening everyone with his yelps. Mark and I found this quite distressing; we didn't like Jack to be frightened or in pain and were glad when this part was over. His prostate was slightly enlarged. It was agreed to leave things as they were and to take him back if blood appeared again.

I phoned Mum to ask what the doctor had said. "I showed him the piece of paper that came with the pills and told him about the side-effects. He took the paper off me, screwed it up and put it in his pocket, saying to 'take no notice of that. Keep taking your tablets, you'll be all right.' Then he went." This really annoyed me and the upshot of it was, Mum stopped taking the tablets, as they made her feel so bad. My brother and sister visited regularly and arranged doctors' visits but she gradually worsened, dying of a heart attack, two weeks later.

I found the loss hard to bear. Once more, Jack had to suffer the long journey up north, to sort out the funeral. Every morning, without fail, Jack would rush downstairs to the kitchen, to look for Mum, not understanding that she wasn't there. After the cremation, the house was packed with neighbours and family for a bite to eat. The dining table was laden with all sorts, including chicken legs and hard-boiled eggs, which Jack almost found too tempting. Luckily, I was called just in time, to stop him from jumping up and pinching a morsel, in front of all the guests. He wasn't bothered by the crowded rooms; the food was uppermost in his mind. I had to be careful to make sure he didn't throw caution to the wind and dive for someone's plate.

With any death, there is a lot of paperwork and bureaucracy. Mark, Jack and I were queuing in a building society. Although dogs weren't allowed in, it was raining hard outside and there was no way I was going to make Jack (and Mark), stand out there getting soaked. I was quite ready for an argument yet no one batted an eyelid, as Jack stood quietly waiting. A lady entered with her little boy, of about four years of age who loudly pointed out, "That dog looks like a big sausage." I laughed as the lady apologised. "It's all right, he is rather sausage-shaped," I said. Soon after, Jack was regularly referred to by us, as a 'cheeky sausage' and a 'lovely little sausage.' He wasn't fat – he just had quite a big gut and when lying on his side, especially after his food, we would say, "Look at this big tummy." A sigh would be heaved and Jack would carry on sleeping, not minding us gently sliding a hand under his belly and weighing it. As long as we were there, that was all that mattered.

One thing Jack was not keen on at this stage was if either of us lent over the side of his big bed to stroke him. He would growl and lunge for us. If his teeth caught my hand, there was no pressure. It was obvious he didn't trust us that much yet and was unwilling to let us into his personal space. I used to say, "It's all right, It's all right," quietly, calmly and firmly, still stroking him.

Another thing Jack would quite often do, if either of us bent down to him when he was lying down or standing, was to quickly snap his teeth together in a resounding clap, a fraction of an inch from the end of our noses. There was no malice intended. Just the opposite, in fact. Jack was teasing us and took great delight in the fact, smiling while waving his tail in the air.

He didn't mind either of us sitting with him when he lay on his duvet, in the dining room. Sometimes, I would sit with him, stroking him, not really thinking of anything. One day, when Mark was at work, Jack and I were together on his duvet, when I idly wondered if he would live to be the same age as Jim had. An awful sinking feeling stabbed into my abdomen. No. I didn't want this feeling. It felt like one of my premonitions but I didn't want to know. I shut it out. Told myself I was imagining things. When I stroked his head, I felt that something would go wrong and it would be in his head. I put it to the back of my mind, refusing to acknowledge it. Never mentioning it to Mark, I carried on as normal.

It was now possible to leave the room without being shadowed by Jack. Not that he was relaxed. Oh no. He would lie there straining his ears, listening to what I was up to. Let's say he was lying in his big bed, in the living room and I had turned the doorknob of the dining room door, to the stairs. Well, he could be by my feet, in front of me of course, before I'd got the door open. And, he had to leap out of his bed, run into the kitchen and through the dining room. There was just no chance of beating him – he was far too quick for that. I figured there was no point in trying to stop Jack getting through the door I was opening. "Wait a minute," I told him. "Mind your toes," I said as I opened the door, his feet being so close in his eagerness to get through before me. Once open, I left it open so that Jack could see I wasn't sneaking out of the front door. He would always fly up the stairs, to watch me. I always explained to him whatever I did. He seemed to like being included and being allowed to share.

Leaving the door open was a turning point. Jack soon stopped running upstairs and quite often waited at the bottom, or wandered off to lie on his duvet. I would always tell him if I was going upstairs, thus leaving the door open, or, if I was, "Going out for a minute. I won't be long," then the door would be closed, to prevent Jack escaping into the courtyard, through the front door.

Well, he did 'escape' through the front door on one occasion. Something had dropped from an upstairs window. Jack was with me on the stairs already and so was with me when I opened the front door. As I peered out, the fallen object was too far away to reach. Like an idiot, I told Jack to, "Stay there." Did he? Did he heck. He scampered merrily past me as I retrieved the fallen article. "Come here Jack," I said, "Let's go in." Not a chance – he was having far too much fun. Skipping and dodging me, as I tried in vain to catch hold of him. Looking through Gill and Henry's windows – oh, how interesting. Oh, there's Gill and Henry; I know them. Scamper, scamper. Whoosh, past Mummy – easy. Like a fool, I started to get a bit annoyed, raising my voice. Would you go to someone who shouted at you? No. Nor did Jack. Running to and fro, he looked through Betty's windows, our other neighbour who was elderly. Ooo, there's Betty. Wheee, off he went, disappearing round the corner of the house. Before I got more than a couple of feet, there was his cheeky face, looking excitedly at me through Betty's lounge window. Betty, sitting there, looking rather startled. How embarrassing. I ran round, to find Betty's door open, which explained how he got in and I apologised to Betty, as I led Jack out. Luckily, Betty didn't mind the intrusion, as she loved all dogs. I did explain to Jack that he shouldn't go into people's houses uninvited. It didn't make too much difference though. He was just so cheeky but that was part of his charm.

If I happened to touch the back door key, no matter where Jack was in the house, he was guaranteed to be at the door long before I could even get the key into the lock. I decided to use the same principle as with the dining room door and would let Jack into the garden, if I was popping to the garage or just putting something in the bin. He would rush up onto the lawn, to wait at the gate, if I went to the garage. If I was putting rubbish in the bin, he would still rush up onto the lawn and sit down. "I'm only putting something in the bin," I would tell him. "Are you coming in?" No. He would have a stroll round the garden, since he was out there. I would close the door and when he was ready, he would let me know.

On the date of my Father's birthday, it had been planned that any family members, who wished, would meet to bury Dad's ashes. I had looked after the ashes since the previous September, when he had died and been cremated, and now on the 10th April, Mark carried them in his rucksack, as we walked into the Derbyshire hills, above Hayfield.

My sister, Susan and her husband, Malcolm and Leo, their standard poodle, along with Alex, their son and his friend; my brother, Barry, my cousin Carol, and my cousin Mark, all the way from Barbados, had gathered on this beautiful, sunny spring day.

This was Jack's first meeting with Leo and Jack made sure that he was in control. There were a few growls between them, although it soon ended up with Leo licking Jack's ears to death. Jack was kept on the lead, partly due to the fact that he had a bandage and homemade welly-boot, on one of his back feet, due to some stitches to a cut and partly, as this was a new area with miles of hillside and occasional livestock. He didn't mind too much as he liked being with a good crowd and another dog.

Higher and higher we climbed, until reaching a lovely spot with a view overlooking a peaceful reservoir. "Let's put him up there, off the path," suggested Susan. Mark, Barry, Jack and myself clambered up the grassy slope, beneath the trees. Mark lifted the turf, to let Barry start the digging. Then Mark did the rest, the soil being deposited in several careful piles around the hole. This was quite some task, being on a steep slope and made especially worse by Jack, who kept trying to lie down comfortably and not succeeding, due to the gradient. As he fidgeted, he slowly slipped downwards, pushing and paddling with his paws, spreading Mark's careful soil piles and kept filling the hole up again.

I got him to lie a bit further up. Again, he started to slide, as he tried to make himself comfortable. Wriggling and squirming, he gained momentum, even with me trying support him, soil and all, he fell into the 'grave.' It just looked so funny, I fell about laughing and I must say, Jack looked quite pleased with himself as well. I think he was making his point, that a steep incline wasn't the best place to rest. It was a good job he fell in before the ashes had been poured in.

The rest of the ceremony went off without a hitch, with us enjoying a leisurely walk over the hills, past gurgling rivers, Jack staring farm dogs into submission. To our utter amazement, when Mark opened the rear door of the Land Rover, Jack leapt straight in and flopped down to rest. Was this a flash in the pan? Was he just tired and glad to lie down? I know I was glad of a rest.

Every two weeks, for many months, we would travel to Mum's house on a Friday afternoon, to sort through loads of hers and Dad's possessions, returning on a Sunday. Jack was a Trojan; coping with all the travelling and not getting the long walks he was used to. We would take a few turns round the field across the railway, where Jack amused himself by teasing the local dogs.

A medium-sized mongrel was chased, tripped deftly using one paw and sent rolling across the grass, emitting a squeak. As I apologised profusely to the lady owner and she told me she didn't mind, up got the dog and chased after Jack, who had carried on running round the field. He skipped round his friend and accelerated to top speed, flying round and across the open space. The smaller dog, after running for a while, ground to a halt, to stand and stare in wonder and defeat.

On quite a regular basis, we would meet a young couple with a Doberman male, who was quite worried by Jack's pushiness. The couple were very friendly, not minding Jack bossing their dog. They said all males bossed him about. Continually standing in front of the Doberman, Jack took his freedom away. Sometimes growling, in low tones, Jack never curled his lips back. He didn't want a fight – just to be in complete control.

Jack tried to control us as well. If we were doing something that didn't suit him, he would let us know vocally, then try to show us what he thought we should be doing. For instance, gardening. Jack couldn't understand why we should be grubbing about on our hands and knees or pruning shrubs. He would curl up on the lawn, looking thoroughly miserable. "I really can't see the point in all this. I'd rather be indoors, in my bed. Mummy and Daddy should come in, so I feel secure and can have a good sleep. Mer, mer, mer," he would whine. "If you don't want to be out here, go in the house," I would tell him. "Mer, mer, mer. I want you to come in too," he would say. "We're not coming in. We've got work to do. You go in and lie down, you'll be all right," I would say. It was no use. He didn't want to be in the house on his own, probably because he thought he couldn't keep his eye on us. Maybe we would sneak out of the garden without telling him. Whatever his reasons, he remained with us in the garden, looking quite haughty and disgusted that we wouldn't do what he said. His pseudonym became, The Black Controller.

Because Jack hated being left alone, we would take him into town, when we did our shopping, on a Saturday. He was pleased to come with us yet at times got a bit fed up with it all. It wasn't ideal but it did save him barking and howling, just in case we heard him, therefore bringing us back to join his company, or so he thought. We used to ask our neighbours how he had been, if we had left Jack and they would tell us he had howled and barked on and off, although there had been some quiet moments. The one very good thing was that he never touched anything, while we were out and he was very clean.

In town, Jack behaved impeccably and was admired by many, looked eagerly into shop doorways, down alleyways and met other dogs, who were also out shopping with their owners. One of these dogs was a polite and distant whippet, which sat by its owner's feet. Jack gave it a hard and unceremonious prod in the chest, with his nose, nearly unbalancing the little dog, which had a startled yet indignant look on its face, (as did the owner). Jack had forgotten that he was not wearing his muzzle and didn't need to push his nose to the end, to be able to sniff at something. He realised what he had done, seeming a little taken aback himself. He didn't like to bash his nose about and made sure he didn't do anything like that again.

Our bread had to be picked up from the bakers, which also had a café. The building had two doorways; one to the shop, which I entered and one to the café, which is where Mark and Jack stood watching the world go by, while I bought the bread.

On one particular day, a lady wearing a red fleece was chatting to the girl behind the counter, while waiting for her bacon sandwich. As I was being served, the sandwich was handed over and the lady in the red fleece left the shop. I finished my transaction and also left. On putting the loaves into Mark's rucksack, he asked if a lady in a red fleece had been in the shop. "Yes," I replied. He told me that she had walked past them, smelling of bacon, then changed her mind, turned and walked back past. The bacon sandwich, in its flimsy bag, was now on their side. Jack, like a crocodile launching itself at a wildebeest at the waters edge, lunged forward. Mark pulled the lead, as soon as he realised what was happening. Jack's teeth made a loud snap, as they closed onto thin air, missing the sandwich by a hair. The lady looked round, only to see a man standing in a shop doorway and a greyhound looking up the road in the opposite direction, as if nothing had happened. She looked puzzled and confused, as she walked off, not quite sure what had made her turn round. We had a laugh about what could have happened, and then went on to the pet shop, to buy a sack of wild birdseed. As it weighed about 20 kilos, Mark couldn't carry it and we left it in the shop, arranging to drive round to pick it up.

Mark pulled up outside the shop. I turned in my seat so I could hold onto Jack, to stop him from jumping out onto the road. I had my arms around his back legs, as Mark opened the rear door of the Land Rover. Jack's nose was in Mark's face, his tail waving in mine. The sack of seed was slung on one of Mark's shoulders. As it started to slide, when Mark tilted it forward, Jack remembered the tins of dog food falling, just missing him and in one movement, he had leapt into the front and was sitting on my knee. He had the memory of an elephant – anything that caused pain or was a near miss, was etched on his brain for eternity.

"What are you doing here?" I asked him, as I folded my arms around him. He didn't answer. Just sat there, ears slightly back, whiskers bristling like a seals and eyes shining in a, "Oh, this is quite good, I like this," sort of way. His hocks dug into my legs but he refused to jump into the back, even though the sack was by the back door and lying flat. "Well, we can't block the road. We'd better drive home like this," I told Mark. Jack's nose was nearly in Mark's left ear. I held on tightly, as we drove through town, along narrow lanes and onto the estate. It was quite obvious that Jack was enjoying this novelty. I sincerely hoped he wouldn't repeat this, as he was crushing my legs. As we drove through the main car park, Jack knew we were nearly home and stood up. I couldn't see a thing, although it was a great relief to my legs. Jack kept putting his head in Mark's way, as he looked at people and dogs in the car park. It was all Mark could do to drive round to our parking space, without crashing into something. Blow me down; when we came to a halt, Jack sailed into the back – no hesitation and waited at the door. "Mer, mer, mer. Right, let me out now." Well, the cheeky sausage.

The birdseed was scattered daily, onto an area of lawn, so that we could enjoy watching the birds. As it was broadcast, Jack would wander round eating all the maize flakes. I'm quite sure he didn't find them particularly palatable. I suspect he worked on the assumption that if they were freely available, he may as well eat them.

If for some reason, Mark and I both popped into the garden, leaving Jack in the house, he would jump up to look out of the kitchen window, making high pitched barks of indignation, at not being included. Then all would go quiet as he dived into the cubby-hole, where the sack of birdseed was kept, top rolled down. Head in sack, he would wolf down as much seed as he could. If I caught him, he would reverse at top speed, as I said a loud, "OUT." Seed and grain peppered everything, filling boots, Wellingtons, strewing the floor and trailing Jack to his duvet. He would lie down and look at me, contrition written on his face. If I didn't catch him, I ignored the fact and cleared up without saying a word.

Jack hadn't eaten the seed because he liked it. He'd eaten it as a small revenge for us not including him in our activities. The results of this thieving were scattered in piles of very seedy poo, around the Deer Park. In fact, more seed than poo. Whether they ever germinated, I'm not sure.

Jack's sack of biscuit meal was also in the cubby-hole and I would occasionally find him, head in sack, crunching away. He soon came out when I told him. We stopped him helping himself, by folding the top edges of the sack together and scrunching them up. Jack couldn't see the biscuits but he could smell them. By being covered like this, Jack accepted that he shouldn't pinch them and never attempted to break into the sack.

In mid May, Mary told us of a nightingale that had come to sing in a copse, by her cottage. Never having heard a real, live nightingale, we elected to combine Jack's evening walk, with a stroll across the park, to Mary's, to listen to the avian vocalist.

Having been such a warm day, the cool evening air was agreeably comfortable for Jack, who really didn't relish being too hot. He always enjoyed Mummy accompanying the evening walk and usually saw it as an excuse to do something different. It was nine o'clock and the moon rode high in the sky, as we tramped through the lush grass. Long before we drew near, the little bird's silvery notes floated to our ears, across the stillness. We approached to within a few feet, then stood spellbound by his beautiful, rippling voice. "Look at Jack," I whispered to Mark. Jack cocked his head from side to side, as he looked towards where the bird sat, in an oak tree, as he too listened to the amazing sound. As we turned to go, he seemed pleased that we had included him in our visit to the little concert and we made our way home through the growing darkness.

In our garden, we left two oval or kidney-shaped areas of grass, to grow long. One had clumps of wild primroses and snakes-head fritillaries, scattered throughout. The other was mainly grasses and yarrow. They added structure and interest, as the breeze waved the long stems and they sheltered grasshoppers and crickets. The fritillaries were a particular favourite of mine, their bell-shaped, nodding heads, hanging from slender stalks; some chequered purple, some white – so delicate.

Jack had been part of our family for about seven months. No longer did he rush round the garden in a panic but revelled in the space – all his – and the opportunity for a bit of cheek and naughtiness. There were shrubs and trees on the lawn, a small S-shaped bed near the back and small raised beds on either side of the steps, one containing a large Escallonia. High hedges down each side with large Rhododendrons and huge trees, at the rear, surrounded the whole.

Jack took great delight in running madly round the garden. Down one side, thunder, thunder, across the lawn, zing; round the back of the wild flower area, (our name for the long grass, primroses and fritillaries), in a tight curve, accelerating out of it; brakes, brakes, brakes at the laurel, zmmm, down the side again and for a bit of variety, charging in any direction in the centre, jumping the bed, dodging trees – I can't look – round and round the conifer bed four times; stop; pant, pant, pant. Off again, round the conifers, only in the other direction. I was surprised at the sharp turns he chose to do, the way he just seemed to love banking over and the challenge of a difficult manoeuvre.

Suddenly, Jack had disappeared. Where was he? "Jack," I called. "Ooh!" I exclaimed, as he jumped out of the conifers, sporting a very mischievous look on his face. How on earth did he find room in there? They had been planted as dwarf conifers yet, as usual, had grown rather large and tightly packed. I was still wondering how he had fitted in, when he leapt in the air and was engulfed by the conifers. "What are you doing in there?" I asked, laughing. The trees shook, as a whole, like a big jelly, with whatever activities Jack was carrying out, when he popped like a cork from a bottle, out of the opposite side. "Hello, you cheeky sausage," I said to his beaming face and waving tail. "This is such good fun," he said, turning and jumping back in, to emerge from the side he had originally entered.

It was such good fun that he had to have another tear round the garden. "Oi, not in the long grass," I called. He knew he wasn't to go in the long grass but when excitement prevailed, caution was thrown to the wind. The swine. His small, narrow feet acted a bit like scythes and my fritillaries had their heads all neatly chopped off. I'd waited all year to see these pretty flowers – now, gone in a second. I didn't tell Jack off; it was up to me to protect anything I didn't want destroying. Mark made some guards from chicken wire and bamboo canes. I took Jack out and showed them to him, so that he knew where they stood and so he wouldn't be taken by surprise when running at top speed. As usual, he sniffed and sprinkled his wee on them and started to kick up the grass, just to make his point." "No," I said, "No kicking on the grass." He gave me a look from the corner of his eye, then shot off for a few circuits, to end up in the conifers for a bit of digging. The conifers became known as Jack's bushes.

I went back into the house, leaving the back door open for Jack to come in when he was ready. As I busied myself, Jack flashed past me, through the kitchen, nails clattering on the lino, straight into the dining room, to make a flying leap onto his duvet, so that he slid along the floor. Leaving the duvet in a heap, he came back into the kitchen to tell me what a fine time he'd had. "Look at you. You're covered in bits of old conifer," I said as I brushed them off with my hands and gave him a hug. "Let me straighten your duvet," I told him, just as he was about to lie on it as it was. He let out a sigh, as he settled into a contented sleep.

I looked down at Jack and thought that when we put a carpet in the dining room, he won't be able to slide on his duvet anymore. I felt sad that one of his little joys would be taken away and imagined the first time he would run in and jump on his duvet, once the carpet was down. I visualized the duvet not moving and Jack falling on his nose.

Well, we put a carpet in, to make it more cosy and do you know what, the first time Jack ran in and jumped on his duvet, it didn't make any difference whatsoever. He still slid across the room. It made my day.

CHAPTER 4

Injury

Mid May was very warm. It was fortunate that I still kept Jack on the lead, as he felt the heat dreadfully. We plodded round lethargically, the wood quiet and still, apart from some birdsong, looking forward to returning to the cool interior of the house.

The interior didn't stay cool for too long, due to my decision to experiment and try making granary scones. Jack slept on his duvet, while I busied myself rubbing in, rolling out, cutting and baking. There were about fourteen in all, smelling delicious on the cooling rack, as I washed up at the sink. Looking through the window, I spotted a wood mouse in difficulties on the lawn. What on earth was it doing? My curiosity got the better of me and I had to go out and have a look.

No sooner had I touched the keys, then Jack was there. "I'm only going in the garden. You've got to stay here," I told him. "Mer, mer, mer. I want to come with you," he argued. "No. You stay here," I said as I squeezed out of the door. He was most indignant.

As I walked up the steps to the lawn, I expected the mouse to shoot off but it crouched with its head down a vole hole, its body totally exposed. I squatted nearby, pondering, deep in thought. How unusual for a wood mouse to be out in the open, in broad daylight. It didn't look injured, just very slow and confused. Happening to look up for a moment, I caught sight of Jack through the kitchen window, feet on surface, pinching a scone. The little blighter. I was down those steps and through that door before you could say Jack Robinson. "Leave it," I shouted. Quick as a flash, Jack had all four feet back on the floor, though looking extremely guilty. He retired to his duvet. No more was said on the subject. I took stock of my scones. The cheeky monkey had eaten three. I suspect this was a bit of revenge because I hadn't allowed him into the garden with me. I regularly left scones to cool and he never touched them. Hmmm. Next time, I would tell him before hand, that he mustn't touch any food items on the kitchen surface. He obviously approved of them though; otherwise he wouldn't have been so greedy.

That evening, heavy rain fell, making Jack very reluctant to go out with Mark, for their last walk of the day. Unsurprisingly, they weren't too long and Jack was very restless on his return. Mark explained that Jack had wanted to sniff in some long grass and he had let him do so, assuming it was a dog scent that interested Jack. Taking Mark unawares, Jack suddenly

1 Jack at the unveilling of the village sign

2 Jack on folded blanket and sheepskin

3 Jack lying in his cardboard bed, listening to Mark upstairs

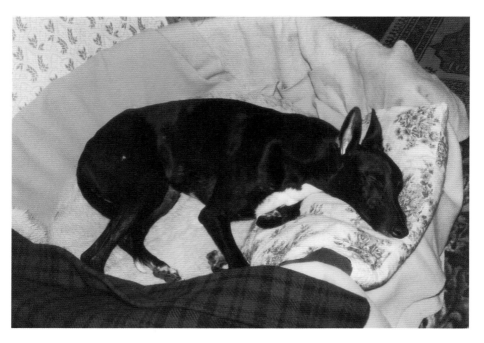

4 Jack in his big bed

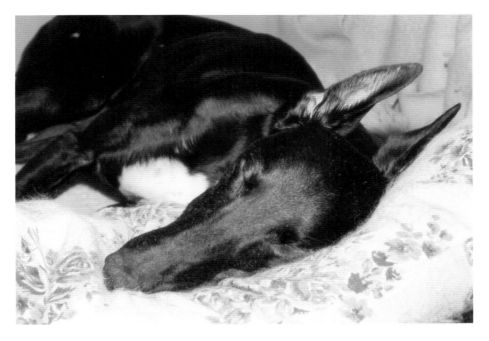

5 Jack in his big bed; close up

6 Jack giving one of his looks

7 Jack sitting by the fireplace

8 After the burial at Hayfield, Jack plus bandage and welly-boot

9   Jack after his tail injury

10   At Mum's burial. Note the almost crossing ears

11 Jack receiving hands-on attention

12 Jack and me at Harlech beach and dunes

13 Collapsing every now and again for a rest at Shell Island

14 Lying in the garden, scenting the air

15　Jack and friend

16　Me with Jack in ring at dog show

pounced, coming out with a young rabbit. He had already killed it before Mark tried to prise his jaws open, which is no mean feat, I can tell you. Eventually, Mark succeeded, throwing the rabbit away.

Never mind the pouring rain, Jack cried at the back door. He just would not settle, wanting to go looking for more rabbits. Not that we let him. We all went to bed. The next day, Jack chased a rabbit, wildly across our garden, the rabbit escaping through the hedge, Jack pulling up short. Oh dear, I could do without more encouragement from the rabbits.

The last weekend in May, an offer was made on Mum's house. We crossed our fingers and hoped it didn't fall through; we would be glad not to have anymore bi-weekly trips up north. Our spirits were lifted.

This jubilation wasn't to last long. Thirty-six hours later, we were making our way round the Deer Park, early on Sunday morning, relaxed and happy. A Springer spaniel rushed madly round, in and out of the undergrowth, looking for rabbits and pheasants to flush out. Jack shot past us at near forty miles per hour. Wow. He looked incredible. On reaching the spaniel, he found it wasn't interested in him, so he left it to its own devices. Mark and I had both said hello to the dog's owner; a man seemingly not wishing to communicate with other dog-walkers.

As we left the Deer Park, somehow we did get chatting to the spaniel's owner. When we reached the point where we would walk to our house, the man suddenly became extremely interested in the fact that we lived on the estate. He seemed to want to chat for ages, even though it was raining. As we stood about, I held Jack on a loose lead. I stood a little behind the man, when Jack unexpectedly, walked round the front of him. The next thing I knew was that Jack was screaming and screaming. "I thought he was going for my dog. Maybe my dog bit him," the man said, quickly stepping out of the way. I stared in disbelief. One moment a bright, happy Jack, a second later a small, crouching figure; head down, tail limp. In fact, he seemed to shrink. I felt sick. All the restaurant staff came out to see what the noise was yet I was hardly aware of them. Mark and I searched Jack's body, especially his neck and shoulders, for bites but found none. A dog going for him would not have produced this effect though. I squatted down. Why was his tail so limp? Redness caught my eye, on the edge of his anus. As I touched his tail, to lift it, Jack screamed again. I soon let go. His anus had been rubbed raw and I could only assume that his tail was broken, at the base. I voiced my opinion that the lead, which was wet and stiffened, being cotton webbing, had got caught under his tail, thus causing these injuries. The man hurriedly made some noises and left.

We walked slowly, as Jack was in intense pain and shock, to our house, where I immediately phoned the vet. Why was it always a Sunday, when these things happened? I was glad it was our vet who was on duty. "Bring him in straight away," he said. I couldn't help shedding a few tears at the thought of Jack losing his beautiful long tail, which he always held so high.

It was so long, and being so limp right now, it very nearly touched the floor.

How would we get him into the Land Rover? He couldn't possibly jump in, he was in such a state. Mark couldn't lift him the usual way, with an arm round Jack's front and the other round Jack's buttocks. This would touch the tail. It would have to be one arm round the front and the other under his belly. A position which Jack hated. He was in so much pain, I don't think he cared and in he went, with me for company and support.

What a depressed dog, along with a frantically worried husband and wife. After a half hour journey, Jack was lifted down from the Land Rover, to walk, zombie-like into the surgery. It was thoroughly impossible to carry out any kind of examination, with Jack conscious. We left him to be x-rayed and examined under general anaesthetic. It was lucky that our walk had been before Jack had eaten his breakfast.

On the way home, we discussed how the injury could have happened. "He was in front of the man. I couldn't see what happened," I told Mark. Silence. I carried on talking, wondering how the lead could have pulled Jack's tail up, when Mark broke in, "I saw the man get hold of the lead and pull it up quickly, then Jack started yelping." "What!!" I rounded on Mark, "Why didn't you say anything at the time?" "It all happened so quickly and I wasn't sure at the time. I think he thought Jack was going for his dog, so he yanked hard on the lead," explained Mark. It all fitted into place. I wondered why the man seemed sheepish and wanted to retire quickly – because he knew he's caused a serious injury. "It's a good job I didn't see him," I blazed, "I would have punched him." More silence. "I hope it's not broken," said Mark. "So do I," I replied, "Although it could be a very bad sprain. I really hope it's that, and not a break," we desperately told each other.

At home, we set to with small jobs; Mark rubbing down a window frame, me filling in small holes and both fitting a new, wind-up door bell, trying to keep our minds off Jack's tail. When 3.30p.m. came round, we set out for the vets.

As we sat in the waiting room chatting, we could hear Jack whining. The vet told us, Jack had been on his feet, waiting, as soon as he heard our voices. When he was brought through, he wagged his tail, ever so slightly. What a relief to see that wag. The vet explained, showing us the x-rays, that there were no fractures. It was badly bruised and Jack needed rest and painkillers. He had had an epidural, which is why a tail-wag was possible. It was a very sleepy Jack I supported, on the way home.

Once in the house, he was glad to be home, looking for his food straight away. I let him have half a tin, then gave him the rest at around 9.30p.m. With the after affects of the anaesthetic and the epidural, Jack had a comfortable night.

The next day was a Bank Holiday Monday and I was glad Mark was there. Jack was suffering, even with his painkillers. He didn't like anything to touch his tail or us to hug him, getting quite grouchy, going for us and wanting to be left alone. So we left him alone. He became very depressed.

It was so sad to see his distress and difficulty, when trying to lie down. As he couldn't move his tail, it hung limply, getting in the way, causing severe pain as it dragged on the floor. Going for a poo made him cry out in agony.

In the afternoon, we decided to have a quick look at a craft fair, which was being held in the grounds and took Jack along for a stroll. We hadn't got far, when a stilt-walker strode up, dressed in black and white. As she loomed over us, I couldn't make out why she wanted to know if Jack's coat was soft and speaking in a high-pitched voice. I was aware that Jack was pulling backwards, legs shaking uncontrollably. I couldn't understand the girl's persistence. We were all backing off, Mark and I trying to shield Jack, when a member of the public, laughing, made a comment about Jack being right to be frightened. The girl was dressed as Cruella Deville, I noticed, as she disappeared with giant strides. I found her stupidity and thoughtlessness hard to comprehend. Jack had been reduced to a complete wreck. We took him straight home, to peace and quiet.

Over the next few days, we noticed small movements in Jack's tail yet it still wasn't evident whether he would regain the full use. We even bought him a Bio-flow collar, as we had heard that they may speed healing. Both of us had a bracelet each, in the hope that they may help my back and Mark's joints.

Jack had moments of enjoyment, in his depression. He came with me to post a letter in the village and on our way back, we crossed a field of tall grass, head-high on Jack. He loved it tickling his tummy, wanting to gallop about but having to accept being on the lead. It was warm and sunny, and pleasant to enter the wood, to walk slowly round. Before we could get home, we met a couple of Jack Russells who were lose and not heeding their owners. Growling and snarling, they raced straight for Jack, jumping at his throat, competing with each other. Poor Jack wasn't his usual self and backed off, nearly sitting down. His confidence was zero at this time, after all, he couldn't signal using his tail and he was in a lot of pain. The man and woman tried to say sorry to him. He didn't want to know, avoiding their advances assiduously. I gave the couple my opinion, quite clearly yet politely; they were most apologetic.

Jack was happy at home where he was safe, entertaining himself in the long grass areas. (Yes I know he knew he shouldn't go in there. After all, he was depressed). Snorting and snuffling in vole-runs, he would stand with one front paw up, nose pointing earthwards, turning his head one way, then the other, ears pricked trying to locate the sounds. Like lightening, he would pounce, using his front feet together and on one occasion, he successfully caught a vole, which, as I stood open-mouthed looking through the kitchen window, he chewed and swallowed, as though it was a Dolly

Mixture. It was like watching a wolf or coyote; very educational really.

Before we went our summer holiday, Jack had a couple of check-ups with the vet, who still couldn't be sure of the long-term outcome of Jack's injury. "Carry on with the tablets," he said, as he handed over a fresh supply. "If he improves, cut them down to one a day, then one every other day. Only time will tell." We hoped Jack would cope with the long trip to Wales.

At an unearthly hour on a Saturday morning, we three, tramped round the wood in mist and damp, to stretch our legs prior to spending most of the day in the Land Rover. The rain came down, as we set off, remaining with us for the entire journey. Well into Wales, we stopped at a mill selling woollens, clothing, slippers and sheepskins, as I reckoned on there being a toilet. I was bursting. Thankfully, there was.

Just inside the entrance, sat a mound of gorgeous sheepskins, which I found impossible to tear myself away from. Mark patiently waited while I sifted through them, looking for the biggest, deepest and silkiest. Finally, a huge dark brown skin, looking like it had come off the back of a bear, seemed to be the one I kept going back to. "Do you think we should buy this for Jack?" I asked Mark. "He's got a sheepskin," he replied. "I know, but he needs another for when I wash that one," I implored. "All right then," sighed Mark. Whilst paying, we asked the sales assistant if there were any walks nearby, to take Jack. "Oh yes, to Arthur's Stone," she said, describing it as though it was quite a slog.

After stowing Jack's sheepskin in the Land Rover and getting Jack out, we strode down a small track, with a burbling river on one side and willow withes on the other. Jack happy to sniff and stretch his legs, a break in the rain, a ray of sunshine and the trilling of a few birds; how pleasant and relaxing. After ten minutes, rounding a bend, there was a standing stone in front of us. "Is that it?" I said. "I think it must be," rejoined Mark. "I got the impression it was a long walk," I remarked. "Well, it might be to her," declared Mark of the sales assistant. We both agreed, it was nice though and fortunate that it was there at all. At least Jack got a little walk.

We arrived at the cottage about 2.15p.m. Rain, rain, rain. It felt chilly. Our accommodation was at the rear of a three hundred year old farmhouse. Rain dripped in, in places. As long as it didn't drip on the bed, I didn't mind. Once the central heating was on, it was toasty.

Jack's duvet was placed on the living room floor and he immediately positioned himself on it, to watch the proceedings, as Mark walked back and to, bringing everything in. Jack's old cardboard bed, now his holiday bed, was put in the bedroom. On my sorting it out, I discovered that we had left his sheepskin at home. "We'll have to use his new one," said Mark. "Of course," I said, rushing to find it and unwrap it. Well, how luxurious. It completely filled the bed, lining the sides and over-flowing. What with his big cushion and travel rug, he looked like a prince. Let's just say, Jack slept very well that night.

Sunday started a little cloudy, then turned into a beautiful, sunny day. Just right for burying Mum's ashes. The family had arranged to meet in the small, coastal village of Borth-y-Gest, which we had known since childhood. A favourite place of Mum's, she had always wanted to live there when Dad retired. Of course, that never came about.

Susan and Malcolm turned up on time, along with Leo, Helen and Alex, my niece and nephew and friends of theirs. As we ate lunch, we discussed where Barry and family could be. Their car was parked not far away. No sign of them. "Typical," we all joked.

Half an hour later, up they strolled, Amelia, my four-year-old niece, in the fore. Helen stepped forward to greet her. Amelia neatly avoided Helen, making a beeline straight for Jack, who gave her a quick lick on the cheek. Well, that was it for the day; where Jack went, so did Amelia. Jack had to be in front, the whole time we walked, while searching for a suitable spot, and so was Amelia. She hardly left his side. Garreg Goch was the spot, with spectacular views along a rugged coast, with beautiful sandy coves and views across the estuary. Everything went without a hitch; no falling in the grave, just panting in the sun. By the end of the day, after our farewells, Jack and I were shattered. Bed was the only place that was of any interest.

The next few days were spent exploring the area. Jack wouldn't allow Mark to pick him up, to put him in the Land Rover, squeaking out every time Mark touched him. From then on, Jack jumped in himself. As there was nowhere nearby to let Jack off, we drove to Harlech beach, after tea. We wanted to see how Jack fared with his tail. We climbed up into the dunes, Jack enjoying the freedom, the soft sand and new scents. As he scampered about happily, I was glad to note, he was using his tail more. He even ran into the sea to have a drink, finding it rather distasteful, so had a paddle instead. As the water got higher up his legs, Jack lifted each paw high, to step over the waves, then shot out of the sea to race round and round the beach, eventually flinging himself down in utter exhaustion, on the sand.

On another attempt to find somewhere nice to walk, we came across the ubiquitous stiles. Greyhounds and stiles do not mix, nor do they 'do' bridges with slatted bases, through which it is possible to observe whatever is below. Neither do they 'do' open stairs and are highly likely to step off a plank bridge.

Anyway, whilst trying to find a way round the stile, we were wondering whether we could paddle round the end of a dry stone wall, which ended in a river. As I moved forward, to have a look, Jack, partly due to impatience and partly due to the fact that he liked to be in front, stepped into the water. Sploosh! Down he plunged, right up to his chest, a rather surprised look on his face. The river was full of large boulders. Luckily for Jack, his legs had slid in between them. How easily he could have broken a leg. We hoisted him out, giving up on the walk and returning to the Land Rover, towelled

Jack off. I made a mental note to keep Jack on the lead near rivers. He didn't seem to mind wading in water.

On the Wednesday, my cousin Carol and her friend, Eric, visited and we walked down to Shell Island, which is full of incredible wild flower meadows and huge sand dunes. Jack thought the dunes were superb, running madly up and down the steep, loose sand, collapsing every now and again for a rest. When we reached a beach, crowded with people, Jack went to bother every dog he could see, until we turned off, to make our return to the cottage and a hearty meal.

On that holiday, Jack had refused to jump in the Land Rover and not wanted to leave the cottage, towards the end of the week because he wasn't getting his usual amount of daily sleep. He had been bitten by wood ants, paddled and waded in sea and river, run madly in the dunes and, wonder of wonders, used his tail more and more. Now he needed a good rest; sleeping for most of our journey back east.

The roads were so quiet, we arrived home by lunchtime and while Mark unloaded, Jack and I went for a walk in the woods. It was time to try him off the lead, without Mark being there. Muzzle fitted, off he trotted. Our walk was full pelt, to every previous squirrel location, with Jack launching himself at each little grey beastie that foolishly stayed on the ground too long. He was getting good at this game. If he had not been wearing his muzzle, he would have caught one. I decided I would leave it a little longer with Jack on the lead, as we returned home hot and breathless.

Shamefully, the next morning, we surfaced late. Our pre-breakfast walk was really mid-morning but as it was a Sunday, it was quiet. We met a man with a black mongrel. The man obviously didn't want to walk the same path as us, nor to let his dog meet Jack. I let Jack off the lead. Both dogs got on fine. "Toby," the man called, sounding quite annoyed. We ignored the man and walked our intended route, which turned out to be his intended route also. He turned back, to avoid our company. As our route was circular, we bumped into the man and Toby, again. He hurried off, as soon as he saw us, down a path parallel to ours. I am always puzzled by the few dog-walkers who stringently avoid other dog-walkers and who expect their dogs to be equally anti-social.

Jack knew that he could meet us further on, if he followed the other path, so joined the man and his dog, whether the man liked it or not – the dog certainly didn't mind. Mark and I called Jack. I didn't approve of him going off on his own, so was relieved when he appeared from an adjoining track, looking pleased with himself. He liked to get away with as much as he could.

For the past few days, Jack had been picking up ticks, left, right and centre, from the church field, from the sheep, and in the woods, from deer. All methods of removal were either not successful or took an awful long time. I had tried Vaseline, Dettol, liniment, a heated skewer – albeit, extremely carefully and methylated spirits. Although meths was the best, it wasn't wonderful, taking around ten minutes to remove one tick. As we were taking Jack for his final tail check-up – four weeks on and tail perfect – we bought a pack containing two plastic tick removers rather like small crochet hooks, one large and one small, hoping they would do the trick. They turned out to be brilliant, taking just seconds to evict any tick from virtually any crevice.

CHAPTER 5

Dog Friends and Squirrels

It was lovely to be back in our woods again, constantly meeting the dogs and their owners that Jack and I had become acquainted with. Sheila, with Dinky, the wire-haired Parsons Jack Russell bitch, who was about fifteen years of age; tiny, very slim and sprightly, were among the first. Little Dinky ran up to Jack but Jack panicked; thinking he was going to be attacked, reversed, then leapt out of her way quickly, leaving her surprised and confused. He did realise his mistake and waved his tail. I found he usually avoided a small dog, if it ran up quickly.

Most days saw us bumping into Daisy and Jaffa, both dogs having an understanding between them, mostly ignoring each other, although on odd occasions I noticed a spark between them. At weekends, when Jack was off the lead, sometimes Jaffa would stand in the path, as if not to let Jack pass. A cheeky gleam would enter Jack's eye, as he stood about three feet away. Suddenly, Jack would either skip round Jaffa or virtually jump over him, at such speed, taking Jaffa by complete surprise. One minute Jack was in front, the next, behind. Hmmm. Er, yes. Mmm. I could almost hear Jaffa saying to himself. This sort of silly stuff from Jack, did earn him some respect; a big dog able to make quicker movements than smaller dogs, or any other type of dog for that matter, does make an impression on those other dogs.

When we first met May and her young, rescue golden retriever bitch, Megan, the young dog had not been spayed and soon came into her first season. It was a good job Jack was still on the lead, because her scent made him go wild. I knew when she'd been in the wood, as he would drag me along, with his nose to the ground, following her odour. It was a great relief when May had her spayed. Jack then gave Megan a different sort of attention.

He would growl excitedly, chasing and knocking her about. This worried May and Megan. Thankfully, Jack soon lost interest, leaving Megan in peace, as long as she didn't run about with Lucy, another golden retriever bitch. When Megan and Lucy played, Jack wondered what they were chasing and thought he may as well join in, usually getting a bit rough, spoiling things somewhat. Not that he meant any harm – he just got a little excited. Even this behaviour didn't go on for too long, allowing Megan and Lucy to chase and play, unhindered, while Jack did his own thing, which was quite often, lying in the long grass while I chatted with Megan and

Lucy's owners.

May, who loved all dogs, carried some dried dog food in her pocket, to hand to Megan or as a small gift to any other dog she met. Jack refused these offerings for many months and would not allow May to touch him. I think he suspected that May was trying to lure him close enough for capture, so he kept well out of the way.

In time, as Jack got used to May, he deigned to accept the occasional piece of dog food and the odd pat. That was as far as it went though. No liberties were tolerated. May, one day made the mistake of putting her arms around Jack's neck, to cuddle him, only to find that he reared up and tore himself from her grasp. Only Mark and I were permitted such luxuries.

By now I was letting Jack off the lead, on most of our walks. If Taxa had recently walked a track, leaving a scent of testosterone, Jack would be off in pursuit, like a rocket, leaving me running and calling, somewhere behind. Bob would wait for me to arrive, panting, Jack bouncing up and down and talking, in a growly sort of way, to Taxa. Occasionally, when Jack met Taxa, he would put on a fantastical performance by springing into the air, all four feet off the ground at once, changing his direction mid-air, so that he landed facing the opposite way. This would be a continuous action, accompanied by his tail lashing like a whip and his greyhound growl. Flinging himself about, he looked most extraordinary yet extremely athletic. Rowan would sometimes be the recipient of this sort of Jack's attention too. It was usually when Jack felt like a bit of excitement and was feeling full of himself; basically, he was just showing off.

Taxa tried hard to ignore Jack. Sometimes Bob and I would walk together, for a way. Jack would then be less confrontational, both dogs sniffing scents, doing their own thing. If we stopped to say goodbye, Jack would go into pester-mode again. It's not that Jack didn't like Taxa; he did. He liked to spend time with him, he found Taxa exciting and interesting.

A dog who found Jack exciting and interesting, was Gemma, a cross-breed with whippet and border collie, in her lineage. Owned by John and Jenny, two lovely pensioners, Gemma adored Jack. She thought he was wonderful, racing madly around him, each time they met. Adoration from any dog, male of female, always pleased Jack. Graciously accepting the attention, he would skip out of the way, if it got a bit too much.

Jack idolized Myrtle, the lurcher bitch, owned by Sally. Myrtle had Labrador somewhere in her breeding, was fawn and smaller than Jack. Her companion was Mila, a smaller still, black lurcher bitch. Even though both were spayed, it was love at first sight, when one day, Myrtle appeared from nowhere to stand at a path junction, framed by trees. She and Jack stared, spell-bound by each other. I didn't know where her owner was nor how far she was going to go and I didn't want Jack haring after her. He started in her direction. "NO," I said, firmly, "This way." This had to be repeated many times, as I could see the turmoil in Jack's mind. "Shall I follow this female, or should I go with Mummy?" I could visibly see him wavering. Myrtle cantered off. "NO. This way," I told Jack, who impressed me no end, by coming with me.

Shortly, we met Daisy and Jaffa, stopping for a chat. We were soon interrupted by Bruno, a border terrier cross, who galloped through our midst, closely followed by none other than Myrtle. This was too much for Jack. He attached himself to the train and had soon disappeared round the next corner. "Bye Daisy," I called, as I chased after them. Eventually, I caught up Bruno's Mum, who was looking after Myrtle and Mila. Jack was happily trotting along with the crowd. He so loved to be with other dogs. After accompanying them until our paths diverged, I was surprised and pleased when Jack came with me straight away, praising him and telling him what a good boy he was. I never forgot to praise any good behaviour, on his part.

George, the Airedale, worshipped Jack. As I talked to his owners, George would scamper and trot round after Jack, wanting to play. Jack never played with other dogs and studiously tried to avoid George, moving further and further away, much to Georges' disappointment. Poor George would come back looking so crestfallen, while Jack stood waiting for me in the distance.

One dog who did make Jack play once, was Taz, a black Labrador cross, who had survived being knocked down by a train. She tore round him, running up to him, then dashing off. At first he refused, knowing that running in the wood, could result in an injury. Eventually, temptation and the desire to show his speed off, got the better of him. He went bonkers, flying round in a big circle, in and out of the trees. I cringed; there was so much debris on the floor. A small yelp sounded, Jack pulling up, limping. Oh no. "What have you done, lovey?" I asked Jack, who then sat, lifting his left front paw to show me. "Ah. You've cut your little leg," I told him. "Mummy will make it better. You shouldn't run about like that in here, you know you always hurt yourself." Mmm. I know, he almost said, ruefully. He was happy, once I had looked at it, remembering not to run about through the trees anymore.

Once home, Jack lay on his duvet, as requested by me, for the purpose of first aid, which was always carried out in the one place. Out came the Listerine and Negasunt, which kept Jack's wounds free from infection, healing any cuts or tears in record time.

Although Jack still viewed our walks as hunting trips, he was calming down and not rushing wildly from area to area, yet still our pace was a fast trot. No longer did Jack fly madly at every squirrel he spotted – if they were too far away, he judged pursuit a waste of energy and didn't bother to break his stride. It was a different matter if he surprised one close by. Even if it was to the side, Jack could change direction in an instant and many was the time he would plunge his front half, into the brambles, in an effort to catch an escaping squirrel.   Normally, Jack wouldn't consider touching the vicious thorns of a bramble but adrenalin and the closeness of his quarry, pushed him past his boundaries.

If a squirrel ran up a tree, occasionally Jack would watch its progress, waiting for a short time, just in case it decided to come down again, or even fall out of the tree, both of which he had experienced.   In his view, if it had happened once, it could happen again.   Thankfully, he never stood there barking.

In our garden, Jack still thought he had more chance of catching squirrels, dashing madly up the six steps to the lawn, sometimes slipping and knocking a leg on the concrete or just clipping a frost-shattered pot, cutting himself.   Many obstacles were removed, in an effort to prevent such accidents but only time saw a change in the manner in which Jack traversed the steps.

The number of squirrels that had to run for their lives, in our garden, grew considerably as Jack's fearless and determined chasing saw him turning on a sixpence, braking at full speed and sliding along on his side, as a squirrel shot under the Rhodies.   One thing I noticed was, the faster the dog, the faster the squirrel.   Sometimes I was in stitches, as the squirrel in question criss-crossed the lawn changing direction, each time with Jack firmly glued to his perpendicular tail.   What amazed me was that Jack never over-shot and always slammed on his brakes at the Rhodies.

Some of the squirrels decided it would be preferable to run up our Mulberry tree, leaving Jack dancing about below.   Eventually, as they were unable to descend, a flying leap would be executed, in an effort to reach either the hedge or the Ribes and Rhodies.   They quite often fell just short and evaded death by inches, scrambling out of Jack's way just in the nick of time.

The vast majority of our visiting grey squirrels all looked the same, apart from the odd ones carrying battle scars.   One in particular, must have been bullied mercilessly, as both his ears had been bitten off.   His name became No Ears, obviously, and I was quite fond of him.   The times that the chasing and treeing of squirrels occurred, was mainly as we re-entered our garden after a walk.   One time, as Mark and I were bolting the gate, Jack had already treed his squirrel.   Joining him at the base of the tree, we all looked up, through the branches. Neither Mark nor I were fans of grey squirrels and Jack's enthusiasm was beginning to draw us in.   With there being three of us on the floor, the squirrel panicked and leapt wildly into the air.   Jack very nearly caught him, as he hit the ground, managing to end up with the tip of his grey tail in Jack's jaws.   Jack spat this out, as the squirrel disappeared under the Rhodies.   Having just caught a glimpse in the confusion, I recognised the squirrel as No Ears and was very glad he got away.   We never saw him again, which led me to wonder, just how many squirrels which narrowly escaped Jack's jaws, did re-visit, or were they different, inexperienced squirrels?

Although fearless, with regard to squirrels, Jack did not like flies at all. They worried him. Even to the point of ignoring a bowl with some sardines, which I'd just put down for him to eat. If a blue bottle buzzed noisily round, that was it. If he couldn't catch it and eat it, up the stairs he rushed, to find sanctuary in the bedroom, away from the small but relentless irritation. First he would check behind the wardrobe. All quiet there. Next, the windows and curtains. That seems o.k. Then a general listen to the room for any buzzing. All quiet. Good. Phew, peace and quiet. Feeling safe, he would lie down and drift off into sleep.

Brrring, went the doorbell. "Woof, woof, woof," shouted Jack as he swarmed down the stairs. There was nothing that would keep him upstairs, if I was opening the front door. He had to be there to keep an eye on things. Smiling at the postman, he waved his tail in the air as he said hello. Our post in, we went into the kitchen. "Jack, do you want your sardines?" I asked him. "Oh yes. Hold on a minute," I could see his brain turning over, as he glanced round the room first. "Mmm. Seems quiet enough. O.k. then." I smiled as he licked the bowl clean. He was such a sweetie.

Cats were viewed differently to squirrels and flies. Having never seen a cat until he visited my Mum's, Jack had no idea what they were and seemed to accept them as some sort of dog. Until, that is, the day when the cat belonging to my Mum's neighbour, leapt up Mum's apple tree and jumped nimbly around, from branch to branch. Jack suddenly took more interest. Tree, fluffy animal, long tail. Was this some sort of squirrel?

This disappointed me somewhat, as we had been trying to encourage a cat down Mum's road, which was used to dogs, to say hello to Jack. Although fearless of Jim, my first greyhound, this cat was not so confident when it came to Jack. With the cat sitting on a wall, we were talking to it and to Jack, hoping it wouldn't run away. Jack sniffed the cat, which smacked his nose with its paw, but with its claws sheathed. Jack accepted that this meant, "Don't take liberties." The cat stalked off.

Our own neighbours, Gill and Henry, have a female cat, Baggins. A male cat, from the village had decided to make its way across the fields to Gill and Henry's, where it lived for some time. This cat was called Tigger and was virtually identical to Baggins, both being dark tabbies. Tigger was slightly fatter and more used to dogs. Baggins resented Tigger muscling in to her home and fought with him whenever they came into contact.

As we returned from a walk, one time, there was a commotion in our garden. Jack being off the lead, rushed to investigate. I was just in time to see Baggins disappearing through the hedge and Tigger, being too fat to fit through the sheep netting, backed up against the wire, facing Jack. Jack, tail waving in the air, was waiting for Tigger to run. "No," I said sternly, "Leave it." Tigger started batting Jack on the nose, which made Jack pull back. "No," I kept repeating, giving Tigger time to make a break for it.

48

Jack did chase him but not with any serious intent.

On one occasion, as we entered the waiting room at the vets, a cat sitting in a carrying cage with an all round view, smashed its way out of the cage, as Jack walked past and climbed up its lady owner, biting her as she tried to catch hold of it, then nearly climbed up the wall. Jack was completely unaware of the cat and its escape.

He did meet another cat at the vets and proved that he didn't see them as prey. This cat sat in its basket, on a lady's lap. I was chatting to the lady about greyhounds, as she was interested in Jack. Jack went forward to greet the lady, with his ears folded back, head level and tail wagging level. He also went to say hello to her cat. They both sniffed each other's noses gently, with no sign of fear or aggression. The lady was most surprised and told me that her cat didn't normally like dogs. I can only conclude that the cat must have seen no threat in Jack's body language. Needless to say, I was very pleased with him and gave him much praise.

A cat did stalk Jack once, while in town, which really made him nervous. I was ready to chase it off if it got too close, as I had heard stories of cats attacking dogs. It seems obvious that animals do read each other's body language very well.

Mark had arranged a days holiday, to enable us to go to the Norfolk Show. Typically, it turned out to be cold and wet and saw us all wrapped up in our rain gear, traipsing round looking at the same stalls as the previous year, in exactly the same places. One of the reasons for going, was for Jack to meet a lot of dogs outside his usual environment. It wasn't tremendously busy, due to the weather and Jack wasn't too pleased to be there, not paying much attention to other dogs, regardless of sex.

Falling into conversation with a couple, with two whippets, we stood under an awning to shelter from the rain. Jack was vaguely interested in the dogs yet his mind was on other things – like, why are we here? I'd rather be in our woods. Suddenly, BANG, BANG, BANG. We all jumped. Shotguns. Jack leapt to the end of his lead, legs shaking uncontrollably, eyes staring wildly. The whippets didn't bat an eyelid. We stood close to the other dogs, in the hope that it may calm Jack, but as more shots rang out, it was obvious that we had better move as far away from the noise as possible. Jack knew which way to go and we calmly walked to the other end of the site, leaving soon after, as none of us were particularly enjoying ourselves.

Although we regularly heard shotguns while walking at home, they were at a distance and had never bothered Jack. Would this incident alter things? We hadn't had Jack for a year yet, but I had observed him closely and found him to be highly intelligent, imaginative, very observant and prone to making assumptions. I feared that when he next heard shotguns at home, he would assume they would at any moment, come close and therefore he would become worried. Unfortunately, this proved correct. Even the most distant of shots was picked up by those radar ears, making them point backwards, tail down, trotting hurriedly along in front of me. "It's all right," I would tell him but he wasn't taking any chances. In time Jack found that the shots didn't move closer and tolerated them with more ease. Thunder was a little similar. Mind you, that could be loud or quiet without much warning. It never bothered me, so we still went our walks, whatever the weather. "It's all right, it's only thunder," I would constantly tell Jack, in a happy voice. This comforted him, giving him confidence enough, in time, not to be too bothered.

It was on one of our regular bi-weekly trips up to my Mum's, Susan and I sorting through stuff, spread all over the floor, Jack lying amongst everything, when I noticed blood dripping from his penis. Oh no, not again. My heart sank, as I feared the worst. What if he'd got prostate cancer? I couldn't bear to lose him.

Back home, I made an appointment to see our vet, who wasn't available until the following day. Meanwhile, Jack seemed perfectly happy, chasing rabbits in the garden, digging in the bushes, finding an old greenfinch – a cat-kill – dead for some time and bringing it in to put on his duvet. "Oh no, don't bring things like that in lovey." I told him, removing the bird and putting it in the compost heap.

Later that evening, as I made our meal, Mark cut up a variety of fresh fruits, making a lovely fruit salad each, covered in creamy yoghurt. Mmm. Placing these on the coffee table, in the living room, he decided to take Jack out for his walk before we ate, due to the fact we were already quite late, as it was. I carried on with the main meal.

They weren't too long; I suspect because Jack thought he might be missing something – of the edible variety. Jack's lead was hung up, then Mark took his Wellingtons off. I was still busy in the kitchen when Mark popped into the living room, to catch Jack's little pink tongue on one of my strawberries, wiping off the creamy yoghurt. "No," said Mark. "Jack's just licked yoghurt off one of your strawberries," he told me. The little monkey. I went in the living room. Jack's eyes caught mine, then dropped to the floor. Very quietly and reproachfully, I said, "Oh, Jack, that's naughty." His head dropped, crestfallen. Walking slowly to the wall by his bed, he stood facing the wall, head down. Just in front of him, a small piece of the old wallpaper protruded. He took this in his small front teeth and absent-mindedly, peeled it off, letting it fall to the floor, standing there overcome with remorse. "Don't laugh at all," I instructed Mark, as we both left the room. Jack spent tea time quietly in his bed and was later rewarded with some broccoli florets, which were happily chewed with great relish, now that he was forgiven.

Very early the next morning, I was explaining to the vet how I'd found blood dripping from Jack's penis. "I'll just check his prostate then," he said. Oh great. "I don't think he'll be too keen on that," I said. And he wasn't. "No one's putting their finger up my bottom ever again," was the message we all got, as he yelped and screamed, jumping around, making the examination impossible. "I suspect, since his tail injury, that he expects a lot of pain in that area, especially by other people," I suggested to the vet. "Mmmm, possibly. I'm not going to be able to examine him like this. I'll give him an injection to shrink his prostate. If it is the prostate, the bleeding should stop. If it keeps bleeding, then it's something else." Thirty millilitres of Tardak was given, which would mimic castration. I wondered if it would alter Jack's behaviour.

He seemed his usual self in the woods, with other dogs and on hearing a yipping and yapping of a distant dog, he stayed with me, instead of running off to find it. He stayed with me, as I carried on down the track, although was in front as usual, when he quickly dived, head and shoulders into the undergrowth and snuffled about. "What on earth's he messing about at now," I thought, when a hare exploded out, a few feet away from Jack and ran towards me, veering off into the brambles when my presence was noticed. I suspected the yipping, yapping dog had been after the same hare. Jack still had his head buried, quite unaware of the hare's flight. I was glad. By the time he looked up, everything was calm. "Come on lovey," I said as I patted him and we resumed our walk.

Out of the blue, Jack decided he was going to spend a night with us, for some reason and chose to lie by Mark's side of the bed, on the floor. His ears flapped every time he shook his head, he snored on and off and muffled barks denoted a dream or two. How many times he woke me, I don't know. Mark slept like a log – never heard a thing.

Our house, which comes with Mark's job, was measured up for central heating. This was a very welcome happening. The buyer for Mum's house had signed. What a relief. Then, more blood from Jack's penis. Oh, not again. Obviously not from his prostate. The blood was so red, I began to be suspicious and examining the inside of Jack's penis sheath, (the prepuce), I found an ulcerated patch, seeping blood. After keeping my eye on it for a few days, a urine sample handed to the vet was found to be clear. "I'd like to operate to remove the ulcer for a biopsy," the vet told me. "O.k.," I said, feeling much relieved; once the ulcer was gone, it would be normal again.

Two days later, Jack had his operation and at the same time, his ear tips were examined, as they were going crusty, with hair loss. No ear mites were found, so a steroid cream was given to me for twice-daily application. Later in the afternoon, we picked up a very groggy, whining Jack, who refused to eat any food and seemed in a complete dream. Poor soul must have felt awful. The next morning Jack passed two black poos in the garden and seemed a little more perky. Still not himself though. His ear tips bled, leaving blood on the kitchen wall, each time he went for a drink. He only ate half his food and then only if I hand fed him. He chose to shorten his walk and didn't go into his big bed, until late evening.

He was still a bit whiny, the next day but the following day Jack was back to normal. Our main walk was a little late in the afternoon, which made me a bit nervous due to Mary telling us the previous day, about two Staffordshire bull terriers that had attacked Rowan, at that end of the wood, late afternoon. It was one of those lovely sunny, quiet evenings, when everyone has gone home. As we approached a bend, with Jack a few feet ahead, two Staffies trotted into view. One a very dark brindle, the other a dark chocolate. Straight sway, I knew it was Rowan's attackers. The bitch went off to sniff, by the side of the track. The male met Jack head on. Jack being a lot taller, towered over him, curving his body almost to form a letter 'C' around the other dog, every muscle standing out, neck arched like a stallion. So much for the Tardak injection. Jack's posturing was all the provocation the Staffie needed. Snarling, he leapt at Jack's shoulder. Instantaneously, the bitch shot in from the other side, to Jack's other shoulder. A whirling mêlée ensued, of black, chocolate and brindle. Growling and snarling, it moved across the track. "Stop it," I shouted. The man who owned the Staffies, bravely stuck his foot into the middle of the fight and somehow managed to grab his male. Mark quickly grabbed Jack, who beamed and panted, waving his tail in the air, looking very much as though he'd had the time of his life. As he had been wearing his muzzle, he couldn't have inflicted any damage to the Staffies, who both looked a little shell-shocked. Jack had no bites at all; they had just bashed their jaws along his shoulders, not using their teeth because Jack didn't use his, nor did he show any fear. I think he greatly surprised them by his speed and tenacity. Jack probably didn't realise the possible danger of the situation and likened the experience to the finish of a race, where some of the greyhounds pile in for a good scrap but with the safety of muzzles. He didn't expect to get hurt. Or was he just glad to be feeling better after his op? He might have felt good; I was shaking so much, I could hardly walk off.

Some days later, blood appeared at the op. site, which coincided with a veterinary appointment, to remove some of the suture. The biopsy report had come back, with a diagnosis of a Mucocutaneous pyoderma, which occurs on mucous membranes and is an uncommon disease in dogs. Just what I wanted to hear. So, Jack had something rare and it wasn't going to go away. Our vet, having read up on the matter, told us there must be a problem with Jack's immune system and the pyoderma would need treatment for life. Anti-biotics were given for ten days, making no difference at all, with another ulcer forming. From then on, topical steroids were used, occasionally weaning off them but always having to return to their use.

CHAPTER 6

Low Times

Throughout the summer, I had been falling into a deep depression and it was getting worse. Losing my Father during 1999, losing my job due to my back injury, losing my wage, losing the power of earning a wage and losing my Mum. Everything I had previously achieved, fell away. I felt completely and utterly useless. All confidence gone. To top it all, I was in constant pain. By late summer, I was sitting at home crying most of the day, contemplating suicide. I cried because I couldn't face life anymore. If I killed myself, I knew Mark couldn't live without me but he would know why and where I was. I cried because Jack wouldn't know where I was and wouldn't understand.

Mark had a shotgun, in a cabinet. I knew where the keys were but not how to use the gun. Many ways of taking my own life were agonized over on a daily basis. Slit wrists in a warm bath, overdose or blasting my brains out. Twice a day, every day, Mark left for work petrified that on his return, he would find me dead. We were both suffering huge amounts of stress. For me, it was like struggling at the bottom of an ocean, trying to swim upwards towards the light. But, there was no light and I couldn't get off the bottom.

Outside the house, no one would have guessed how I felt, as I smiled, laughed and chatted to people I met. The only person who observed my pain yet wasn't affected by it, was Jack. He was still impatient, demanding and quick to let me know if anything wasn't quite to his satisfaction.

All doctors could offer me, was tranquillisers. No thank you. Having experienced them for two days, in my late teens, I preferred not to be zonked up to the eyeballs and having to be propped up all the time, by pills. A lot of thinking went on in my head. Telling myself that, no matter how bad things were, good would come out of it in the end; it couldn't last forever and to take each day as it comes. I focused on Jack.

Mark and I, both thought a move may help. With us not having our own house, this limited the places Mark could work. Large country estates with representative housing, were the only option. On the completion of my Mum's house, we had a look round a large garden, up north, leaving Mark's details with the Head Gardener, in case a vacancy arose. Applying for jobs, somehow made us both feel a little more optimistic.

Being out of the house, with other people, helped to relieve some of my stress. When we could fit it in and when we had advance knowledge of it, we would attend our parish council meetings. On a lovely August evening, we walked across the fields, accompanied by Jack, to listen to the local business and give our opinion, if necessary. There were more council members than audience, being just Mark, Jack and myself. I had never seen a dog there before and hoped Jack would not show us up. Even though the hard floorboards were the only resting place, he seemed aware that he had to behave and that any conversation must be in hushed tones. The most noise from him was a very quiet whine, which I hurriedly shushed, and was probably to tell me that the floor was too hard. Not another murmur passed his nose, as he tried various uncomfortable lying positions, on the wooden floor. Later, he was rewarded with a chat with Mary, whom he was extremely fond of, lashing his tail wildly when he met her, and who gave him a small dog biscuit, for being so quiet during the meeting. She told us of two young barn owls that she had seen near the wood, which we looked out for on the way home. Sure enough, as we tramped through the dusk, three ghostly forms flew across our path and into the wood.

Towards the end of August, the weather was hot with clear blue skies. To lie down and feel the sun's warmth, was better than being indoors. Being about three feet from Jack's bushes, he kept me company, lying in their shade. For some reason, he wasn't happy with me lying down and went into the conifers, to dig and snuffle noisily. "What are you doing in there?" I asked. Out he backed, tail waving, covered in bits of dead conifer, which he vigorously shook all over me, then ran madly round the garden a few times, before retiring indoors. Which all made me smile.

The next day, was a repeat performance, only this time Jack tried to remove a low branch, which was obviously in his way, inside his bushes. Not only was he covered in bits but I had to clear bigger bits from his mouth. If he was trying to gain my attention, it certainly worked. It also took my mind off things, a little.

Early the next day, as we returned from our walk, Jack found a dead lamb, which had expired during the night, lying against a fence. He trotted towards it. As he got no reaction from it, caution overtook him and he approached slowly. One front paw was extended to touch it. Still no reaction. He went into a play-bow, waving his tail and barking. Laughing, I told him, "It's not going to play with you, lovey, it's dead." Over the next few days, until the lamb was removed, Jack paid it hopeful visits. Little things like this brought small pockets of joy into my life.

Mark went kickboxing once a week, which helped him escape the stress for a while. Jack and I stayed at home. One particular evening, we were in the living room, watching television, when we heard one of our back gates and footsteps. Jack and I looked at each other. Leaping up, I went to look out of the kitchen window, into the dark, Jack on my heels. Just making out two police disappearing up the garden, I left the light off and quickly opened the back door, hooking my fingers under Jack's grab-collar. Calling to them, brought the policeman and woman back down the garden, to stand at the top of the steps. Whilst I enquired as to what was happening, Jack launched into a loud and vigorous barking tirade, ears erect, probably looking quite fearsome. The police did not come any closer. After satisfying myself that all was fine, I thanked them and off they went. Closing the door, I praised Jack to the skies for 'protecting' me. He was magnificent.

Reading about a fun dog show, to raise funds for retired greyhounds and border collies, we decided to enter Jack. It would be a good day out and an opportunity to meet other greyhounds and their owners. The venue was a community centre in a village outside Norwich, with a large grass area with stalls, show ring and obedience section. Jack was entered in Best Short Coat, Most Handsome Dog, Dog in Best Condition, Dog the Judge Would Most Like to Take Home and Best Greyhound.

As we walked round, prior to the showing, one of the judges admired Jack greatly. Unfortunately, it was the wrong judge; he was judging the obedience. Our judge was a young girl who obviously had the idea that greyhounds' ears should not be erect, quite plainly showing that she thought Jack ugly, almost passing him by in the ring, nearly forgetting to examine him. And this was only in the first category! As she was judging all categories, I could see we would just have to go through the motions, as Jack was not likely to be picked at all. He was ignored in favour of dogs with dull coats and long nails and mostly, dogs that belonged to friends of the judge. I'm quite sure Jack understood, just as much as I did; he made a point of cocking his leg on the barrier-post, each time we left the ring.

The day was an absolute scorcher and when not in the ring, we sat with Jack in the shade of a friend's car, with a good supply of water. Regardless of the judging, we thoroughly enjoyed ourselves, meeting and chatting to other greyhound owners. Jack was especially happy, being in company with so many dogs.

On our return home, we took Jack a walk, as he'd been denied a proper one all day. Through the car park and into the field in front of the farm, full of sheep, a yearling lamb, hand-reared, trotted towards us bleating noisily. Jack glared, going into stalk mode. "Hello lamb," I called, holding my hand out. Ignoring Jack completely, the lamb came for a sniff and a stroke. Jack looked quite disgusted, walking behind Mark to stand surveying the horizon, probably a bit miffed that his stare hadn't worked. Probably a little self-conscious too, so pretended that he wasn't really bothered. Leaving the lamb behind, we went our walk.

Once again, my depression took a turn for the worse. Life was a living hell. Mark came home with an advert for a job on a large country estate, many miles to the west. I phoned for an application form, which arrived very quickly, was duly filled in and posted off. A few days later, I received a phone call to make a date for Mark's interview.

The date arrived and the interview went so well, that it was certain, Mark had the job. Another date was made for him to meet the owner of the house. On this day, it was confirmed the job was his.

Early October, a week in Morfa Bychan, North Wales, was taken, in the hope that it would do us good. Another luxurious sheepskin was purchased for Jack; well, he was such a good boy. Our accommodation, this time was one of many bungalows, on an estate on the coast. Although, a beautifully furnished property, the central heating didn't seem to want to warm up. Warm, was all it got and due to the cold, wet and windy weather, I was frozen. The owner brought a plumber round, to fit a new pump. Jack lay on his duvet and barked at them, if they entered the room. With a new pump fitted, things did heat up, which was fortunate, as each time we entered the house after a walk, all our coats, trousers, hats and gloves needed drying by the radiators.

My back was awful, due to me tripping at home before our journey, then sitting on a 'directors' chair to try on some waterproof over-trousers. When I came to stand up, I couldn't. It was agony. Most of the holiday, I spent hobbling and shouting out in pain. It didn't stop us walking twice a day, on the beach. Jack pestered us to get up at six a.m., on a daily basis. Once washed and togged up, down the road and take a left onto a large expanse of sand, backed by dunes. Jack would visit any dog visible and was lucky enough, one morning, to meet a lurcher bitch whom he at first, refused to run with. She wore him down in the end and what a sight it was. The sand was damp, firm and smooth, so suited Jack down to the ground. They flew round at top speed, Jack always faster and making sure that he was in front, being so competitive. We could feel the air turbulence as they flashed close by our legs, grains of damp sand flying up into the air. A greyhound that has had a racing career, will usually retain that competitive edge and put more into running, than one that has not. It never fails to give me a buzz.

On the evening walk, on our reaching the beach, we would turn right, entering huge dunes, covered with tall, waist-high Marram grass, not unlike the Pampas. Completely obscured from our view, Jack was off on rabbit scents, never catching any but ever hopeful, re-appearing at odd intervals on distant ridges, then disappearing quickly again. Mark ran after him, while I lagged far behind. Eventually Mark and Jack met and made their way slowly back to me, in a round about fashion, Jack panting, bright-eyed and bushy-tailed; he certainly was enjoying himself.

The dunes backed onto a caravan park, from which a fresh water stream flowed. A wooden plank was the only crossing place. I crossed first, to show Jack that he had to stay on all the way across. Well, he knew better. In an effort to reach the far path and overtake me, he stepped off half way, plunging two feet into the stream, which was one foot deep and full of watercress. "I told you to stay on the bridge," I remonstrated, as he scrambled out and carried on, pretending nothing had happened. For the rest of the week, Jack used the bridge in the proper manner. His problem was, he usually thought he knew better than I did. Gradually, he had to admit that I was worth listening to and learning from, at times.

The next morning, a twitcher had set his tripod telescope up on our usual route. Statue-like, glued to his lens, he appeared a strange figure to Jack's vivid imagination. Huffing, puffing, jumping backwards and forwards, kicking sand vigorously in all directions, Jack challenged this danger. Some tail lashing showed his concern. "Come on Jack, it's all right," I called, stifling my laughter. The silly beggar. Eventually, summoning great courage, he dashed behind the man, to the safety of the open beach.

Always walking to the end of the beach, we rounded a rocky headland on which stood a tiny house. On the far side we would ascend a narrow boardwalk, between scrub, to climb over the headland and return to our original beach on the far side. After showing Jack the way down, he tore off along the beach and disappeared into the dunes. We walked along the beach, every now and again espying Jack, as he had a look to see where we were. Before the bank from dune to beach got too high, Jack joined us, probably to chase a spaniel he had spotted, in and out of the sea, then have a good burn up before going back to the bungalow, for breakfast.

The next day, the walk was the same, except for when we descended the headland, Jack shot straight up into the dunes. Assuming he would make his way along, as on the previous day, Mark and I carried on up the beach. After not sighting Jack at all and being near to our exit, we called out, "Jack. Jack." Nothing. "Where is he?" we asked each other, as we scanned the dunes and beach. "There he his," I pointed, as Jack shot down from the dunes, at the spot he had entered earlier. "Where's he going now?" I said, as, instead of running towards us, Jack scampered off up the boardwalk and over the headland. He couldn't hear our shouts, due to a strong wind blowing from him to us. We both stood in silence. Suddenly, from around the headland came Jack, who flew towards our waving arms, with a distinct look of relief on his face. He had been so preoccupied with his own business, he had failed to note us going up the beach and on his return to where he had last seen us, decided to retrace our earlier route, to look for us. His reasoning certainly worked but it would have been more sensible to make sure he knew where we were, before immersing himself in his own activities.

Carol and Eric paid their usual visit and after a drink of tea and some cheese and olive scones, we went for a walk. Across the golf links and along the coast path to Garreg Goch, with Jack scampering off to explore various side tracks, usually to caravan sites, then shooting back onto our path at top speed, nearly causing coronaries all round to any walker in the vicinity. After visiting Mum's 'grave', a walk back along the beach was voted on. "There's no way Jack can get down there," I indicated to the jumble of rocks on the descent. Carol and Eric were already climbing down. Jack put one paw onto a sloping slab of slate and finding it slippy, withdrew his paw, uttering a small squeak. "You'll have to carry him," I told Mark, "I'll help to support you but we'll have to be careful." Jack never flinched, nor made a sound as Mark gathered him up, keeping perfectly still, as we cautiously negotiated each rock. We reached the sand with relief. None more so than Jack, who after being so brave, dashed round in sweeping circles, in sheer elation, plunging his feet four or five inches into the soft, damp sand. He got so hot, I removed his coat. Off he went again, in and out of tidal pools, looking into every cave. Stopping to cock his leg, he stood in a pool to cool his feet. "Come on Jack," I called. He accelerated forward. Whooshsplash; disappearing into an unexpectedly deep pool, his little face, eyes staring, moved steadily forward, as he paddled furiously to find a footing. Climbing out, water streaming from his back in a waterfall, he stood dazed and sorry for himself, as I went forward. "Ah," I started to say, then changed my mind. "Good boy. What a good boy." A gleam entered Jack's eye. Shaking himself energetically, another mad run of jubilation was partaken of, studiously avoiding all pools of water, of course. Two adventures in one day, was plenty for a greyhound with a vivid imagination, thank you very much.

On our return to the bungalow, I got the meal on the go, while the others prepared the table, then sat down for a chat. Carol had brought apple pie, stewed apple, wine and a herbal fruit drink for Mark and I, along with a Spanish omelette. We already had an apple pie, lots of creamy yoghurt and a huge, warming stew containing everything you could think of. While the stew was heating up, I divided the apple pies into their dishes, leaving them on the kitchen table. Every now and then I would stir the stew, to stop it sticking to the pan. Trying to do everything at once was not easy and I was feeling a little stressed. As I turned from the pan, there was Jack nibbling with those tiny front teeth, at one of the pastry piecrusts. "LEAVE IT," I exploded and chased him down the hallway, to his duvet in the living room, where he stayed curled up very small, for the rest of the preparations. This had the same effect as an alpha male or female in a dog pack, growling or snarling to say, "Don't touch that, it's mine. You can have some when I'm ready to let you have some."

With the meal on the table, Jack lay like a statue on the dining room floor, patiently waiting for his titbits at the end. He thought the stew was pretty darned good, especially being rewarded with a bowlful, for behaving so perfectly, after the crust nibbling earlier.

On the morning of our departure, the rain lashed down. At six a.m., we drove down the road to the beach, so Jack could go to the toilet. All he did was to have a wee here and there and we all got thoroughly soaked with rain. In the Land Rover, I removed Jack's coat and towelled his head and neck, before setting off on our journey. At six forty five, Mark pulled over suddenly to the side of the road, leapt out into the pitch-blackness and was sick three times. Oh no, not now. Vomiting sessions had plagued Mark for some time now and no one could find out what was causing it. When he thought he was all right, Mark climbed back in and we set off, once more. At seven twenty a.m., we were forced to pull over again, into a lay-by, where we ended up for the next four hours, watching the sunrise while Mark brought his food up, at least ten times. Jack took the opportunity to have another walk, the slept soundly.

Gone eleven a.m., with Mark white as a sheet, we set off, the Land Rover windows running with condensation. By mid-day, a blue sky and sun was very welcome. Arriving home at nearly six p.m., the house was freezing. Mark lit the Rayburn, while I took Jack in the church field. We took hot water bottles to bed with us that night, and tucked Jack up under his travel rug.

I must admit, the next day in the woods, Jack looked a picture, his coat gleaming, every muscle well defined, obviously the result of our evening excursions into the dunes.

Readying myself for our move, with Mark's new job, I potted many of the plants from our garden and organised for three removal companies to come and give estimates. Jack barked at each man who came to size up the job, especially if they stood too close to me. He would get in between the man and myself, barking and jumping towards the man, bringing both front feet down on the floor with a thump. I felt safe with Jack around.

The contract of employment arrived in early November. I was doubtful. Had grave feelings. The comptroller rang to set a date to view a house, for a couple of days hence. Making my feelings clear to Mark, we discussed the issue at length. I really felt that the deal there could not compete with the deal here. We would view the house before making the final decision.

After another long trip, we waited by a reception desk for someone to show us to the house. I got the distinct impression, from observing the people who worked there, that not much time was given to anyone. Everyone seemed stressed, rushed, put-upon and talking openly in front of us, about others behind their backs. I was not impressed. We were guided to the house and left to look round. It was far too small for all our furniture, situated on a busy-ish road, nowhere to walk Jack, no garage for Mark's lathe and a lovely view of a motorway from the back garden, constantly droning hypnotically. No thank you.

We sent the contract of employment back. I knew it was the right thing to do. Two days later, Mark was admitted into hospital for the day, to have a piece of bone removed from his left foot. A work colleague saw to the Rayburn for me that evening and from then on, our friend Richard came twice a day to empty the ashes, bring the coal in and take me shopping, when necessary.

At weekends, when Mark would normally come with Jack and I, on a walk in the woods, Jack would try his best to encourage Mark to come along. In the evenings, he couldn't understand why Mark wouldn't take him out, whining and waving his tail in front of Mark, then trotting out of the room and turning to say, "Come on then." He had to make do with me instead.

Two weeks later, Mark tried a Wellington on, after I had changed his dressing for a smaller one. It fitted. Jack was overjoyed because Daddy was taking him out that night. Mark hobbled painfully round until Jack was satisfied. The things we do for those we love!

Mark also accompanied Jack and I on the early morning ramble and the main walk, the next day. Jack seemed to know that he couldn't shoot off and waited as Mark limped along. His foot was so painful the following day, that Mark stayed in and I took the opportunity to remove his stitches. One month later, Mark was back at work although his foot was still extremely painful.

Jack and I went back to our normal daily routine, meeting his dog friends and some new, not so friendly dogs. As we approached the Deer Park, on our way homewards, a girl with a black Labrador male and a Jack Russell male, both on leads, walked towards us. Jack just had to march up and stand right in their faces. The Labrador lunged and so did the Jack Russell. Jack growled and pulled back quickly, only to find the Labs teeth fastened through the wire of his muzzle. The Lab let go but not before the wire had stretched momentarily, under pressure, allowing Jack's lower jaw to be pulled through the other side. "Ow, ow, ow, ow," Jack yelped, feeling trapped. The girl hurried off, whilst I tried to free Jack. He panicked and struggled, continuously shouting. Telling him not to be silly and to stand still, I prised and pulled the wire until at last Jack was free. He showed his relief by pushing his head into me and wagging his tail, to say thank you, seeming a little bit ashamed of his moment of panic and all the noise. Telling him what a good boy he was, I gave him a big hug.

We went into the Deer Park. A woman walked ahead, with a small dog off the lead. Jack went up to the woman, who was quite unaware of his presence. She jumped, shrieking out, making Jack jump two yards to one side. He went to see the little dog instead, who turned out to be old and friendly. Jack seemed quite subdued.

At home, I accidentally knocked the poker over, onto the tiles by the Rayburn. Jack was so jumpy, he squealed out. Poor Jack; it just wasn't his day. Later, I re-soldered his muzzle.

A few mornings later, Jack didn't want to come his pre-breakfast walk, which was most unusual. He did come with me in the end, but was slow and unenthusiastic. Refusing his breakfast, he shivered and lay on his duvet. Covering him with his wool blanket, I found his feet remained cold, his heartbeat irregular and he was quiet all day, showing some improvement later. While holding his feet, I did one of my regular foot-checks and found a long cut on one of his front pads, which I speedily cleaned and dressed.

The next day, he was his usual cheeky self, except wearing a bandage and a welly-boot for his walks.

Some days later, on our early morning pitch-black walk, we saw flashing lights darting round the meadow. Good grief, is it fairies or aliens? We stood still trying to make out what they were. "Woof, woof, woof," came a volley of barking, as two cocker spaniels and a big brown thing rushed out of the darkness. Jack stood his ground. The spaniels were just noisy, not nasty. The big brown thing, turned out to be a curly-coated retriever who was frightened of other dogs. However, he loved greyhounds. Well, he certainly loved Jack. Tearing back and to, bouncing three feet in the air, rather like Tigger, he was beside himself with joy. Jack took it all in good humour, standing still, in complete control yet rather enjoying the adoration.

After breakfast, Jack requested to be let into the garden. "Wait a minute, let me put your welly-boot on," I said, pulling it up and taping it in place. "Be careful and don't run round, otherwise you'll slip," I instructed him. Waving his tail high, he backed up as I opened the door. That cheeky look spread all over him. "What's he up to now?" I thought, closing the door to keep the frosty, cold out. Returning to making sandwiches and chopping salad for lunch, I was soon occupied. Gradually, a drumming, rushing sound, which increased then decreased, crept into my consciousness. Looking up and wondering what it was, my eyes fell on Jack, tearing round at top speed. Rushing to the door, I flung it open, running onto the lawn in my slippers. "Stop running," I told Jack, who looked very pleased with himself. His welly-boot lay on the lawn and his sock, a few feet away. "Come here, you little monkey. How did you get your boot and sock off?" I asked, cuddling him. "Let's go in, come on." Jack cantered into the house and jumped on his duvet. "Lie down. I want to clean your foot," I told him and he duly did so, to have his foot cleaned and redressed. I suppose he was getting frustrated by not going off the lead and by having shorter walks. He needed a burn up now and again and if he didn't get enough exercise, got fidgety in the house and did not sleep as much. As for removing his bandage, that was a one off. Jack never chewed his bandages at all. The most he ever did was to lick his leg above the sock, which I used to cover the bandage, trying to push the sock down with his tongue, as he licked where his leg itched.

A few days later, Jack was liberated from his dressing and boot and off the lead. Ah, freedom again. Meeting friends, chasing squirrels; this is the life. We met a black Labrador male, which we hadn't seen before. Usually, when we met a dog, not previously seen, we never saw them again; they were usually visitors. This one went for Jack, grabbing his wire muzzle and so, pulling his bottom jaw through again. What is it with black Lab males? This time Jack didn't panic as I readjusted his muzzle, freeing him. He kept well away from the black Lab, after that.

On our way through the Deer Park, Jack chased a squirrel and must have hit a branch on the ground, as I later found a half-inch square tear, in the skin of his rear left knee. Far too mangled for stitching, I kept it clean using Listerine. After resting, it had stiffened up, being on a joint. Poor Jack, he didn't half feel sorry for himself. Honestly, no sooner does one bandage come off, then he sustains another injury. Fortunately, this one didn't need a dressing. I suspect that because Jack was so overjoyed to be free again, he just went wild, dashing about more than normal.

His sore knee sobered him up a bit, though he still had his freedom. I used a big nappy pin to pin Jack's coat up, so it didn't rub on his poorly knee. With me cleaning it and with Jack licking it, the tear got smaller and smaller, until it disappeared completely.

Christmas was quiet. Walks in the snow, lighting log fires, having Richard round for a meal. No matter what I did, I still felt depressed.

CHAPTER 7

Dominance, Deer and Foot and Mouth

During most of January, Jack suffered spates of painful spasms around his abdomen, kidney and thigh area. He would scream out either lying in his bed or whilst on his feet and would turn his head towards the painful spot. Mark and I both felt all over where Jack indicated, finding very tight muscles. We got the vet to give him a very thorough check over, with nothing obvious being found. His anal glands were emptied, which made Jack scream even more!

All we could do was to massage his belly, which sometimes seemed to help. I pondered on whether it was trapped wind and suggested to Mark that we try bringing up Jack's wind, after he had eaten. Mark agreed and Jack soon got the hang of being burped post meal times and especially after food and a drink of water. He would stand while one of us rubbed our hands in a sweeping motion, backwards and forwards, from belly to chest, until a large burp was expelled. "That's better," I would say, carrying on until a secondary belch was discharged. Jack found this so relieving, that if he felt he needed help to expel some wind, he would come to stand quietly by one of us and wait. He didn't make a fuss by scratching or crying yet I soon picked up on what he wanted. Whether his pains were trapped wind, I don't know. Since we started burping Jack, it was very rare that he cried out.

It was around this time that Jack bumped into a big Rhodesian ridgeback and a black Labrador, both males. I'd never seen either dog previously and nor had Jack, who pushed himself into them both, although concentrating mostly on the ridgeback, which was bigger than him. I was quite amazed by his recklessness. Tail waving, eyes wide, barging right into this dog. He just seemed too big for his boots. I managed to grab his collar and held on, while the two men accompanying the dogs, could lead them off. The next time we met the ridgeback and his owner, he was minus his Lab friend and Jack took great delight in squaring up to him. At first, this concerned me, as the ridgeback looked as though he could make mincemeat of Jack but as we got to know the dog and his owner, Jack, through his bravado and strutting, clearly had the upper hand. As soon as he got a whiff that a dog was concerned by his presence, (an unneutered male) then he would swagger and pose, showing off his speed and his athletic body to his unfortunate victim.

I was beginning to understand Jack more. Jack's behaviour towards un-castrated males was still dominant, albeit toned down to a considerable degree. Although he certainly looked aggressive, I'd come to realise, after my close scrutiny of him over time, that he was not actually being aggressive.

His body language was that of an extremely dominant dog, yet he wasn't particularly that way inclined. I saw him allow Leo to take a rawhide chew from his jaws, because Leo did not want to share his chews. Mind you, he was in Leo's house.

What Jack liked to do, was control the situation. He had very quickly concluded that being a greyhound, his capabilities far outweighed that of any other non-greyhound male. Thus, he played his domineering games.

A very dominant dog that plays by all the rules, does not attack, as it has no need. Jack never attacked. Nor did he bare his teeth. He growled at times, usually because he was enjoying himself. It was a greyhound growl; not one of aggression.

Sometimes, we came across dogs that didn't play by the rules. These could give out a set of signals to say they were friendly, than act in the opposite way, once close enough to Jack by attacking him. Obviously not confident dogs.

Jack's behaviour limited the likelihood of him sustaining an attack on himself, purely owing to his body language and his posturing. Jack did not stand with his head over another dog's shoulder but always barred the animals' way, by standing stiffly in front of them, showing off how fit and athletic he was. If they dared move off, Jack would be back in front of them in a flash. This worried many dogs, as it quite plainly told them, that they could never escape by running away.

The males whom Jack knew well, who were the recipients of these 'games', also observed as time went on, that Jack meant no harm. Rowan, who understood Jack better than any of the others, used to pretend to be interested in scents on the ground, if he didn't feel like interacting.

Occasionally, when Jack stood right in another males face, the other dog would tell him to go away, with a snarl and a lunge. Jack would then leap out of harms way and leave that dog alone, realising that he was wasting his time.

I suspect Jack played strictly by the rules, because he wasn't removed from his mother at eight weeks old, to be put with humans and given behavioural problems. He grew up surrounded by adult dogs, thus learning behaviour patterns similar to a pack of wolves.

On the whole, the majority of unneutered males deferred to Jack, sending him the message that he was in charge and boosting his confidence. He had certainly earned his title of The Black Controller.

Some of his behaviour did make me wonder if he was ever attacked, during his racing life in kennels, after finding two large scars under his hair. One at the top of his left shoulder, just on his neck, the other on his throat, also to the left. This could explain why he was always watching his back and occasionally, would jump almost ten feet, while sniffing or drinking from a puddle, as if he thought something had crept up on him.

Jack was very patient with ill-mannered dogs. One instance I recall, was a meeting with a lady with a rescued yellow Labrador male, who was very boisterous, wagging his tail, while at the same time jumping at Jack, snarling. I told the lady that he would be better off the lead, so she let him off. He kept jumping at Jack, who growled once and kept jumping back out of the way. The lady became worried and started shouting at her dog. This in turn worried Jack, who then walked off with her dog in tow and stood some distance away. Eventually her Lab was persuaded to come back to have his lead put on. Jack then quietly walked back to me, of his own accord. The poor lady was full of apologies and praised Jack for being 'so good and patient'. "Yes. He is very good," I said. "It looks like your dog has never been socialised. Maybe if you muzzle him like Jack is, then you could let him off knowing he can't bite another dog and eventually, he would learn how to be with them," I suggested. "I don't think I dare let him off again. Not many people are as understanding as you," she said sadly. "Do try it," I replied hopefully, "After all, it's not much fun keeping your dog on the lead for the rest of its life." Her dog obviously had very confused messages, feeling the need to be threatening but was doing so out of fear. He never bit Jack, otherwise Jack would have reacted very differently, by putting him firmly in his place. We never met them again, although I did speak to the lady, when Mark and I met her down a lane, while we were in the Land Rover. We had a chat and she divulged that she had not had the courage to let her dog off again. I felt sorry for her and her dog.

Mark had applied for another job, this time in the West Country. The interview date came round all too quickly. I was not looking forward to the long journey, which I knew Jack would hate.

Up at two a.m., on the M25 by six a.m., we reached the nearest town to our destination by nine a.m. The interview was at a quarter to two in the afternoon. A bit of time to kill then. Typically, as we parked, torrential rain battered down. After sitting there for a while, it didn't look as though the rain was going to stop, so we bravely though reluctantly climbed out of the Land Rover. Quite a busy shopping town yet not too dog friendly, as some privately owned streets banned dogs from even stepping on them; CCTV cameras were apparent to report any canine crimes!

Mark had to visit his bank and although a notice on the door, said 'NO DOGS', there was no way I was going to make Jack suffer any more in the deluge, so I took him in and no one said a word. Not so in some charity shops. In one in particular, I scanned the door and window for a 'no dogs' sign, and none visible, we entered. Suddenly, from the rear of the empty shop, rushed an elderly man and two elderly ladies. "Dogs aren't allowed in here," they chorused. "Do you allow children?" I asked. "Oh yes, we allow children, yes," their faces a little less hard and angry. "I don't know why," I told them, "Dogs are far better behaved!" They all looked as though they'd just sucked a lemon, as I had a quick look round before leaving. We did find one that didn't object to Jack going in and as usual, he was the model dog, meekly, patiently and quietly waiting, while Mark and I sifted through the clothes.

Hunger pangs and time sent us back to the Land Rover, where I removed Jack's coat and rubbed him down with his towel, which he found most welcome. Mark and I sat there soggily dripping, steaming all the windows up, while we ate lunch, giving Jack some eagerly awaited tit-bits and warming ourselves with a hot drink.

At twelve thirty, we drove to a Little Chef, so Mark could change into his interview gear, then sat chatting until shortly before the interview time, when we drove to our destination. Mark went in on time and I was given directions for a riverbank walk, with Jack. The rain continued to fall, much to Jack's and my misery. No matter how closely we followed the directions, I couldn't find the river. The fields were half flooded, as we plodded disconsolately on. "We'll go back when you've done a poo," I told Jack. A few feet further on, he sat down for his poo and no sooner had he finished, then he turned round and led me back to the Land Rover. Had he understood my words? He looked shattered. He was so tired he could hardly jump in. Kneeling in the front, I leant into the back, took his coat off, gave him a good rub down and some biscuits. When he lay down on his duvet, which we always took on long journeys, I covered him up and he fell into a deep sleep.

We waited and we waited. The wind built up to gale force, rocking the Land Rover so violently, I feared we may blow over. I put the radio on and stared out as best I could, through rain-lashed windows. I waited. Jack was in another world, woofing in his various dreams, his feet twitching under his blanket. The light, what there was of it, was fading fast. I was busy wondering how long this interview was supposed to be, when Mark appeared through the dusk, at ten past four. Thank goodness for that. Mark gave Jack a stroke, who stayed where he was, cosily comfortable.

"I'm going to drive back today," Mark told me. "Are you sure you're all right. You're not too tired?" I asked him with slight concern. "No, I'm fine," he assured me and off we went to fill up with diesel. The appalling weather followed us home, slowing our journey. It didn't seem to affect other drivers, who shot past us on the motorway in monsoon conditions, at top speed.

It was one thirty a.m., the next morning, when we hit our beds, sleeping well and not surfacing until ten a.m., which is not like Jack, or me. The first thing we did was walk in our woods, where Jack re-acquainted himself with all the familiar scents.

Mark and I discussed the job interview and accommodation, at breakfast.

The area was quite flat, becoming extremely waterlogged when it rained and having a river nearby, would it flood? The house was tiny, with no central heating and no garage, and very importantly, there was nowhere suitable to walk Jack or let him off the lead. It really wasn't worth it. We decided we would both be better off where we were. So, no more jobs were applied for.

It was at the end of January, that Jack had a close encounter with deer. All three of us were walking down a long straight track in the woods, Jack in front, then me, with Mark bringing up the rear. This was how it usually was. Taking us by surprise, two red deer leapt out of the undergrowth on our left, just in front of Jack and cantered along ahead of him. Initially, Jack started after them, also cantering. As I watched he gradually got slower and slower, until he came to a full stop and stood staring after the disappearing deer. Mark and I had kept our normal pace and coming up to Jack, found him completely rooted to the spot. "Come on lovey. It's only deer," I explained. "No, I don't want to go up there," he seemed to be saying. "It's all right, we'll look after you," I said hugging him and planting a kiss on his head. With his tail down, ears flicking round, especially directed behind and sideways, he slunk along trying to make himself small and looking extremely worried. For the first time ever, he never left our side on a walk and squirrels didn't exist.

Later, in the house with Jack asleep, Mark and I were watching a wildlife documentary, when on the programme, a dog barked at a snooping bear on a trailer park. Jack leapt up out of his bed, rushed up and down the room looking very worried, then went to the back door. I opened it for him. He stood with his front feet just on the threshold, peering into the garden, refusing to go outside. It was obvious the dog on television was telling the bear he was not welcome and Jack, hearing this assumed the deer had come after him and the barking dog was telling them to go away.

A few days later, down a totally different track, at the opposite end of the wood, one in a hollow with banks on either side, two roe deer shot from our left, leaping head height over the path, like the cow jumping over the moon. What a fantastic sight! Poor Jack, he took in their speed and height – something extremely fast, capable of bounding to great heights was something that demanded great respect. He looked shocked and troubled, as we carried on but was cheered up somewhat by meeting his German shepherd friend, Scipio, who adored Jack, gently playing round him.

The next day, Jack shadowed me around the house and then lay in the office with Mark, while he worked, not wishing to be left alone, just in case. As no deer visited our garden or house, Jack soon relaxed and got back to normal, especially rummaging round in the garden in the evening dusk, running at top speed and grubbing about in his bushes, then dashing in to shake desiccated conifer bits all over the kitchen floor; happy and confident once more.

He usually accompanied Mark into the garden to say goodbye, on kickboxing nights, although there were times when I didn't let him do so, as he quite often wouldn't come back in again. Probably because he thought he'd wait for Mark's return in the garden. One night in early February, Jack trotted by Mark's side across the lawn. Half way, Mark stroked Jack's head, "Bye bye Jack, I'll see you later." Jack stood watching as Mark disappeared into the dark, listening for the gate latch. As I watched from the back door, Jack turned then sat down facing the house. Something had caught his attention up above. He sat there, gaze riveted. "What are you looking at Jack?" I queried. He sat there totally absorbed. My curiosity burning, I tiptoed out in my slippers and dressing gown, up the steps and onto the lawn, which had the beginnings of a frost. Following Jack's gaze, there above the roof was a brilliant full moon, every mountain visible. How astounding. I'd never met a dog who noticed things like this before. Squatting down by Jack, I put my arm round his shoulder. "That's the moon. Look at all the mountains," I told him. Gazing for a while longer, he then stood up, quite satisfied that he had built up his knowledge a little further. "Let's go in lovey," I suggested and we descended the steps into the house, locking the door behind us.

By now, reports of foot and mouth had hit our television screen. All cases were in far flung areas of the country and it didn't seem to have anything to do with us. Restrictions looked awful, with families being imprisoned on their farms. As more cases appeared throughout the country, we hoped none would make it this far.

During the last week in February, Jack accompanied us on the Saturday shopping trip into town, as was normal. On our return, as we drove through the main gates, we were greeted with massive barriers of straw bales, scattered straw soaked in disinfectant on the road, and notices instructing people to walk in the wood only and to keep off the parkland. Restrictions were here. "You know, we'll have to leave Jack in when we go shopping. We can't be disinfecting his feet," I said to Mark. "Yes I know," he said, "He won't like that." "He's got no choice," I replied.

Well, he didn't like it, yet surprisingly, quite quickly got used to it. On our return from shopping, Jack would shout loudly, telling us off for leaving him. After a matter of weeks, I detected a distinct change; he wasn't really bothered but pretended to be. One day quietly saying hello, then remembering that he hadn't shouted, started to tell us off, then found it was all too much trouble and effort, so went for a scamper round the garden instead. The silly sausage!

Restrictions got more severe, with residents and employees using the old exit, driving over disinfectant-soaked mats and washing boots in bowls of disinfectant. All deliveries were via the main entrance, where all vehicles had to be sprayed, Mark taking his turn on spray duties. Eventually the woods were sealed off and notices posted on all paths. The only people allowed in were Mark, Jack and myself, along with Mary and Rowan.

Near the end of February, snow fell quite thickly, making the woods a magical place. Jack loved it just as much as we did, running round being silly and making us laugh. The highlight was meeting Mary and Rowan. Jack started by showing off to Rowan, soon progressing to dashing off round a corner, with Rowan in hot pursuit. Whoosh – Jack suddenly shot out again, going straight across, then quickly turning, dashed back just as Rowan appeared. Jack went completely silly, wildly rushing past us, flying round in large arcs, lapping Rowan, who had no chance of keeping up. It was wonderful to watch Jack gallop so effortlessly, covering the ground with such ease.

He was also excited by snow falling in the garden. As I filled up the bird feeders with frozen hands, big flakes of snow fell. The swirling flakes made Jack run round and round the garden, until a bit out of puff he stood waiting for me, snow building up on his back, head and whiskers.

Due to the snow, we could see where people had ignored the restriction notices and walked in the wood. On the whole, people did stay away and Jack became very concerned as the other dog scents faded. He wanted to search down tracks we didn't normally use, just in case he found the comforting presence of dog aromas. He ran to the dog-walker's car park to check if any dogs were there. He was sad and didn't enjoy his walks. The lack of his usual scents made Jack far more aware of other scents, like rabbit, squirrel, deer, stoat and fox. He was a dog who needed to be interested in something.

One beautiful day, at the beginning of March, Jack and I were walking towards home through the Deer Park, which was filled with sunshine and birdsong. I had removed his coat due to him being too warm and he insisted on going down the side which borders a field, because of all the rabbit burrows along there. As I headed for the gate, Jack decided to hop under the barbed wire, where there was a dip in the ground, making his passage easy, into the corner of the field. "Come here, Jack," I called to no avail. Jack was staring into a bramble patch, through the fence that ran from the corner. He then started darting back and to, excitedly. My ears picked up quite a loud sound of an animal in the brambles. What on earth was it? By now I was shouting, "No," and "Leave it." Jack looked very much as if he was about to launch himself through the barbed wire. I'd have to get him. Scrambling under the wire, I rushed forward, still trying to figure out what animal it was making such a din. Convinced it was a fox, I made grab for Jack's collar. He neatly dodged and took a calculated leap through the barbed wire, his head, shoulders and front legs, into the brambles. My heart nearly stopped. He'll be torn to pieces. Simultaneously, out of the brambles on the far side of the fence, shot what I took to be a squirrel in the confusion, which headed into the Deer Park. Quick as lightening, Jack jumped back out of the brambles, between the barbed wire and under the other wire, into the Deer Park, after what he also assumed was a squirrel, which danced around, not going up the nearest tree. As I ran after him in a panic, my brain recognised the creature with a black-tipped tail, as one very angry stoat. "LEAVE IT. LEAVE IT," I shouted, so loudly that Jack did listen but was confused. Why should he leave it? My reason for shouting was not to tell Jack off, as he wasn't being naughty. He was doing what came naturally to him. It was to make him listen and to stop him attacking the stoat. When a dog is hunting, he doesn't hear you – you know, like when you talk to a man who's watching television; he's not ignoring you – he just doesn't hear you!

I crawled back under the wire but my hood got hooked on a barb, stopping me in my tracks. I continued to shout as I frantically tried to free myself, and the stoat, maybe thinking there were two attackers, bounded off. "STAY THERE," I bellowed at Jack, managing to extricate my hood. He did stay there and I was able to put his lead on. I think everyone on the estate must have heard me that day. "Let me look at you," I said shakily, as I checked Jack for injuries and was amazed to find none. He wasn't daft; he knew about barbed wire and had sized up the situation before jumping. Nevertheless, we kept away from that corner for some time.

Some days later, on a very frosty early morning walk, Jack found a rabbit with myxomatosis, just inside a bramble patch. I hadn't realised what he was up to until he leapt in and dragged it out, even though wearing his muzzle. He had pushed so hard, his top and bottom jaws had popped through the wire gaps. How he squeezed the rabbit like that, I'll never know but he killed it before I got to him. Then he found he was stuck, squealing as I prised the wires apart and removed the muzzle, to free him. Once free, he sniffed the rabbit and left it. After second thoughts, he went back. Picking it up, looking very pleased with himself, he trotted proudly into the Deer Park with me, where he paraded round for a while, showing off his rabbit. Having a mouthful of rabbit doesn't make breathing easy, so he put it down eventually. "Leave it," I told him and he did so. Over the next few days, he paid visits to his rabbit, just to make sure it was still there and to remind himself how clever he was to have caught it. I didn't tell him I could have caught it myself, easily.

A few days later, again when we were walking in the Deer Park, I wondered if there would be any more myxy rabbits about and to be on the safe side, I removed Jack's muzzle. I didn't want him getting stuck again. Seconds later, he was stalking a rabbit, which just sat there not moving. It turned out to have myxy and Jack picked it up easily, squeezed the breath out of it, then trotted round proudly making sure that I had a good view of him, tail and head held high, displaying his prize yet not letting me near enough to remove it from his jaws. I stood watching him striding round, expecting him to put it down and leave it. He didn't. He seemed to be looking for a good place to hide it and after some time disappeared behind a large old tree butt, with branches around it. Once he was satisfied the rabbit was safely stowed away, he wiped his face on the ground, then rolled in the damp grass, reminding me of a wolf. I slowly walked round, to see what he had done with his catch. The whole rabbit was stuffed into a small-ish hole, which was well hidden except to the extremely observant.

Jack was so keen on rabbits, he would sometimes refuse to come home from our walk, trotting purposefully off again in the opposite direction. This sometimes necessitated a sternly raised voice, which usually changed his mind but not always, as he was a very determined character. Occasionally, I had to chase after him to put his lead on. One time whilst I remonstrated with Jack not to go off hunting again, as it was time to go home, he sat down. This melted my heart and took any frustrations away. Hugging him, I told him what a good boy he was. I always hugged and praised Jack when he came back to me, either from running off on a scent or to have his lead put on – it was far nicer to be welcomed with kind words and affection than to be told off on his return, which would have made him avoid me at all costs, not to mention, distrust me. It is surprising just how persuasive a hug and a kiss, along with a few kind words, can be.

Deer were becoming more frequent visitors, due to the lack of humans and dogs and sometimes Jack and I would see one in the Deer Park, not far from our house. Poor Jack. Once in our garden, he would stand facing the gate staring in earnest, thinking the deer would follow him home. Then he would stand in the doorway for a final look, still somewhat worried, before allowing me to close the door.

Throughout the wood, many deer tracks were visible in the mud, ostensibly red deer, roe and muntjac. The muntjac and roe rubbed musk from scent glands on their heads, on small saplings, making their presence very obvious to Jack, who lifted his nose to delicately sniff the thin branches. I always knew when deer were not far away, by Jack's body language – the flicking ears, tail more down than up and him scenting the air.

Quite often, on our pre-breakfast walk, we would see groups of deer, a couple of hundred yards up the woodland walk. They would look at us and we would walk slowly up, looking at them. Jack, being off the lead, stayed in my vicinity. The deer quietly slipped away. Jack then took the opportunity to go and sniff where they had been yet would refuse to follow the track they had taken.

One thing Jack wasn't frightened of was squirrels and although he had never caught one, he loved hunting them. His muzzle had prevented any success in that quarter, until the end of March. As usual, on entering the Deer Park on our way home from the main walk, I removed Jack's muzzle in case he found any myxy rabbits. What a beautiful spring day; warm sun, birdsong and primroses. I was miles away. Jack had gone up a rise, behind and to my left. As I strolled down the sloping path, feeling relaxed and happier than I'd been in a long time, a squirrel crossed from left to right, a few yards in front of me. Jack must have been moving already when he saw it, because he shot past me at top speed, to pick the squirrel up and shake it violently. (Something he never did with rabbits).

It all happened so quickly, I was quite stunned. As he trotted round showing it off, I could see its front paws starting to paddle the air. It wasn't dead. I was worried as I watched him searching for a suitable hiding place. After a while, Jack started digging a hole by a fallen log, depositing the limp squirrel in it. Because of the undergrowth, I couldn't see clearly. I could tell that Jack was resting with his front paws in the hole and could see his bottom in the air. Suddenly, loud yelping split the peace. I saw Jack jump about then he was shaking the squirrel in his jaws again and trotting off to look for a different burial place. Knowing it must have bitten him, I couldn't do anything until he had buried it. This time Jack dug a good hole at a tree base. As I approached to look for his bites, he made a grab for his squirrel. "No, leave it. I don't want your darned squirrel," I said as I stuffed my Wellington on it, pulled Jack away, then kicked earth into the hole and stamped it down. "Now, let me have a look at you," I told him. His face was fine but his front left pastern had bites on the front, which must have punctured a large vein, making his leg swollen with loose blood. Oh my goodness! Quickly putting his lead on, I marched him across the Deer Park to a private gate in the fence, which was a short cut to our house. Mark had heard Jack's shrieks and met us as we crossed through the gardens, looking very worried. "I'm going to phone the vet," I assured him.

The vet instructed me to bathe it in salt water and bind it up with a pressure bandage. He said Jack was lucky it wasn't his main artery, down the back of his leg. That made me shiver. I also applied Listerine and Negasunt before binding up, checking his paw didn't go cold which would indicate a bandage being too tight. Jack was totally unconcerned about the whole thing. He wore his muzzle the next day – I didn't want any more mishaps. The swelling had gone down completely within two days, although I still cleaned his wounds until they fully healed.

He wasn't out of the woods yet, so to speak. On a weekend early morning walk with Mark and I, Jack, muzzleless, was on a squirrel tail when it ran up a tree, only to come down again right where Jack was. Utter turmoil reigned. I couldn't see what was going on. When I heard loud squealing, I knew he'd got it and it had bitten him. This time, after shaking it to stop it biting him, he squeezed it to kill it, then took a while to find a good burying place. He was totally worn out when he emerged from his task and this time, he had covered the hole over himself. Checking him over, I found one or two bites on his face. Hunting looked as though it used an awful lot of energy up, as Jack plodded by us for some time. I presumed that would be it for this walk. Sadly, no. Further on, another squirrel must have enticed Jack to chase and we couldn't see him anywhere. We called out, "Jack, Jack." "Here he is," I said as Jack trotted up panting. "Is he limping?" I asked Mark, then I noticed his right rear foot didn't look quite right. The inner toe was sticking out at a right angle. "He's dislocated a toe!" I exclaimed. "Why is it always a Sunday when he needs the vet?" I remarked, putting Jack's lead on. He didn't seem bothered by his toe and walked home without any trouble. He lay on his duvet while I phoned the vet on duty, who told me to 'bring him in'. "Come on Jack, let me put your lead on," I said and up he jumped, trotting over. "Oh, it's gone back in," I told Mark. "He must have knocked it in himself," he replied. Quickly, I phoned the vet back, to tell her. "Sometimes that happens," she said, thanking me for letting her know. "Shall I bind it up for a few days?" I asked her and was told that that was a good idea. After wrapping his foot up, I cleaned the bites on his face.

Bandage or no bandage, Jack had to walk on the lead to rest his toe for some considerable time. He really did not enjoy his walks on the lead and became quite down. All the stopping and starting, as he sniffed here and there, did not do my back any good either. When he met Rowan, he would leap madly about, wanting to run with him but had to stay on the lead. After a few days, I removed the bandage and the toe came out once only. Just as Jack was squeaking in pain, he knocked it back in as he lay down, stopping mid-squeak, as if to say, "Oh, it's stopped hurting." I kept a close eye on him, especially in our garden, as he ultimately became tempted to run round in frustration at not being let off the lead. "Don't run. Don't run," I would call to him and he knew what I meant because he would stop straight away. Once or twice he squealed out as he tried to run. "Come here. Let me have a look," I would say, as he came to show me his foot. His toe stayed in place, thankfully.

Due to foot and mouth restrictions, Jack had now to be kept on the lead in the wood, anyway, so this helped his toe heal fully. A month later Jack was lapping our garden at top speed once more, on his 'race track', which he had worn for himself and which Mark had added sand to. Feeling rather full of himself, he sat down and did a poo right on my biggest clump of primroses, in the long grass area, then did another lap of the garden; the cheeky monkey!

An occasional treat was to be let off the lead, when Jack met Rowan. They would both go completely bonkers, dashing back and to and being totally silly. Jack running off the track into non-brambly areas, Rowan charging in and out of a deep water-filled rut; Jack shooting up and down the 'dip', past our legs, at top speed. Times like this, made life worthwhile.

I now decided to leave Jack's muzzle off full time, partly because I was sick of mending it and mainly because he seemed perfectly fine with other dogs. He was glad not to have to wear it, too. Unfortunately, this meant he could pick up rabbits with myxomatosis and if we were nearly home, he wouldn't bury them but insisted on carrying them home, to bury in the garden. Once I had put him into the house, I would pop out and throw the dead rabbit into a clump of brambles, in the Deer Park, making it impossible for Jack to retrieve.

Although the hall and gardens opened in early May, the woods remained closed, apart from two tracks on the perimeter. I could always tell if people had brought their dogs into the restricted zone, as Jack would be riveted to their scent, sometimes covering it with his own urine and growling, accompanied by vigorous kicking.

Whatever the weather, Jack always went his walks. After the initial, "I'm not going out in that!" when looking out of the door, at the rain slanting down, he would reluctantly step out, appreciating his rain coat yet hating getting his head wet.

Near the end of April, prior to our main walk one day, I could hear thunder rolling round. This didn't bother me, and Jack was quite good by now with regard to a rumbling sky. As it was raining, we were both wrapped in our waterproofs, feeling reasonably protected against the wet. Through the meadow, up the woodland walk, round the back of the farm, below the felled area; thunder rumbled now and again. "Let's go through the beech trees," I said to Jack. Up the sloping track we trudged, heads down. BANG – FLASH! A deafening thunder clap accompanied by a pillar of lightening directly a few feet in front of us, made me jump and Jack shot to the end of his lead, in one massive leap, nearly taking my arm out of its socket. "Mmmm. Right," I said, "Er, I think we'll go this way instead."

Turning, we set off on another route. As we progressed, the volume of rumbling grew less, so I presumed the storm was swinging away. Just as we reached another junction where we were to turn right, BANG – FLASH! Again, a blinding pillar of lightening directly in front of us, making us jump. Was someone trying to tell us something? "I think we'll go this way," I told Jack, as we turned left to head for home. A short way along, Jack wanted to carry on the walk, instead of heading home, which surprised me somewhat. "No lovey," I told him, "We'll come out again later, when the storm has gone and we'll finish our walk then." He reluctantly trotted homewards. I tried not to hurry and not to linger either; this was one heck of a storm. As we passed the donkeys, the thunder was so loud, it made the ground shake like an earthquake.

I was relieved to get into the house and close the back door. Whilst sitting on a chair in the kitchen, removing my Wellingtons, a clap of thunder sounded so loud that the back door rattled violently. I really thought it was going to be blown in. It was like a giant banging on it. Jack and I both stared transfixed, until the thunder subsided and everything went quiet.

Well, there was plenty to do, while waiting for the storm to clear, so I set to scraping wallpaper off the bathroom wall, in preparation for decorating before the central heating was to be installed, in July. Jack chose to lie on the landing, watching me work, while the thunder crashed and the lightening flashed through the window, which I had opened to vent the moisture as I sprayed the paper. It helped take my mind off the weather, although it wasn't particularly good for my back, so I worked slowly until Mark came home and got stuck in with me.

Time had moved on and Jack started to get restless, whining, trying to tell me something. I looked out of the window – quiet, blue sky and sunshine. He certainly seemed to be saying that the storm had gone and as I'd promised to take him out to finish the walk later, now was the time. "I'm going to take Jack to finish his walk," I explained to Mark, "I told him I'd take him out later when the weather cleared up and it has, and that's what he's telling me, so I'll see you later." And with that, off Jack and I went to finish our walk.

Some weeks later, another storm took us by surprise, although not as badly. This time Jack was off the lead behind me, when quite a loud peal of thunder sounded. Jack shot past me so fast, I could hardly call out to him for laughing. "It's all right, it's all right. It's only thunder, you don't need to run away," I told him. When he heard my voice, he stopped and looked at me, then trotted in front, still slightly worried. Thankfully, the storm quietly rolled off, so we finished our walk in peace.

By the time June came round, foot and mouth was still rife across the country and after ringing the owner of the cottage we had booked in the Cotswolds, I decided to postpone the holiday due to the close proximity of cases in our chosen area. So, no holiday; we stayed at home.

Occasionally, Mark and I would take Jack his evening walk, in the woods and let him off, as the days were longer. We generally kept to the narrow dog-walkers tracks and on one of these, one evening, as we turned homeward, Jack stopped in front of me. There being thick brambles on either side, I nearly tripped over him. "Go on Jack," I said, touching his thigh. "No, I'm not going up there," he seemed to say, his ears flicking like mad, tail down, eyes staring. "There must be deer about," I told Mark. Managing to squeeze past, I walked on. "Come on Jack, it's all right," I assured him. Hesitantly he came forward a few feet, then became frozen. "You come past him Mark," I said, "Then maybe he'll come with us." Mark stepped past and we both turned immediately to our right. The deer, long gone by now, must have previously been in a thicket just to Jack's left and slightly in front, leaving a strong scent. "Come on lovey. It's all right," I called, as Mark and I stood a few feet away, facing Jack, waiting. He reminded me of a young horse that wanted to gallop, being reined in – his feet were moving but he wasn't going anywhere. He just could not pluck up the courage to walk a couple of feet round the corner of the brambles. He allowed his fear to take a grip. Suddenly, he burst to his right, tearing himself straight through the bramble patch and ran past us. "Wait Jack," I called. He stopped and turned. "Don't laugh at him," I instructed Mark. "Good boy. What a good boy," I praised Jack as I went forward. Wagging his tail yet feeling a bit foolish, he came for a hug. Praising him again, I told him to stay with us and that it was all right. His courage returned and we made our way home with no further incidents. One thing I liked about Jack was the fact that he was quite good at learning to face his fears and overcome them, although he allowed panic in now and again; that was quite understandable.

On the whole, he was a very confidant dog and also very perceptive. By now, he had got to the point where, when I picked up the back door keys, he knew whether I was locking or unlocking the door. If I was locking the door, he would stay in his bed. If I was unlocking it, he would leap up and have his nose to the door jamb before I could get the key into the lock. He didn't want to be left out of anything.

Jack no longer followed me everywhere. We had a definite routine and he knew what was happening and when. After the pre-breakfast walk, he had his tin of meat, his teeth cleaned and his ointment on his pyoderma and ear tips. Then he retired to his big bed in the living room, where I tucked his rug round him to keep him cosy and to prevent him from licking his ointment off his prepuce.

While Jack slept, I ate breakfast, washed the pots, did my teeth and prepared sandwiches for lunch. I always saved a bit of fish or whatever filling I was using, providing it was suitable, for Jack. Instead of him coming into the kitchen to lie down, while I made lunch, he would stay in his bed until the filling was on the bread and the top slice in place. Only then would he silently appear and have a good stretch, before licking the bowl clean, which I had put down for him. Fish, he found a bit salty, so always had a drink of water afterwards. He would slip away as quietly as he had arrived, either back to his bed or to lie in the corner of the living room, with his back to the bookcase.

Jack's attitude to us leaning into his bed had gradually changed. No longer growling or lunging, he very occasionally gave a rumble at Mark, if he put his face too close, while Jack was lying down. He loved to be stroked and hugged while comfortable in bed. Lying propped on one elbow, reclining against the back of the bed, he would transfix me with a stare, as I sat in my chair, as if to say, "Come to me and stroke me." He was so lovely, I couldn't resist and I would sit by his side hugging him and stroking his soft, silky fur, sniffing his ears and whispering to him. His eyes would close in enjoyment and relaxation. If I stopped, thinking that he must be tired of it now, his eyes would slowly open and a paw would stretch towards me. "Please don't stop," his face would say, so of course, I would carry on. He could take any amount of this sort of treatment.

When we went shopping, or were going out without Jack, he would come into the kitchen to look at me, as I put my shoes on. "No. You stay here," I would say, in a disappointed tone. His little face fell, as he turned and walked into the living room to climb into his bed. "I'll say bye, bye in a minute," I would tell him. Once Mark and I were ready to go, we went and knelt by Jack's bed, stroking him, saying, "Bye, bye. We'll see you later." He looked so sad, as he stretched a paw out to us, imploring us not to go. I hated leaving him and couldn't wait to get back to be with him. There seemed to be an invisible umbilical cord between us.

If we were taking Jack out, any time other than a normal walk time, and he came to see if he had to stay in, I would tell him, "Yes. You're coming with us," in a happy tone and of course, he was overjoyed to be included.

On our return from a trip without him, I would always say, "Hello Jack. Hello little Jack," in a very happy tone, telling him what a good boy he was for not touching anything. He certainly recognised the words 'bye, bye' and 'hello', whether we used them to him or to other people. If I had Jack on the lead and said hello to another person, Jack knew it was a greeting and would go into hello mode – head down slightly, ears flat on his head and tail giving a slow level wag. Sometimes the person was not a dog-person, so would not recognise Jack's body language and ignore him. I would tell him afterwards, "It's all right Jack, they're just ignorant. They didn't know you were saying hello."

There were many words Jack recognised but I'm quite sure that a lot of what he understood was by telepathy. He liked our friend Richard and had visited his house a couple of times, yet whether he knew Richard's name, I'm not sure.

One evening, as Mark was getting ready to take Jack out, we were all in the kitchen, Jack waving his tail and poking his nose between Mark's legs. "I wonder where he'll take me tonight," Mark said to me. Laughing, I replied, "Probably down to Richard's." Not that Jack had ever taken Mark down there, of his own accord. Out they went, while I busied myself washing up the dishes. Time went on. "They're a long time," I thought. "Where on earth have they gone?" Although it stayed light late, it had already gone dark. I strained my ears for sounds of the garden gate, Jack's impatient whine at the door or his rattling the doorknob with his nose.

After some time, my ears were rewarded. "Mer, mer, mer. Let me in for my biscuits," said Jack. In he rushed as I opened the door, Mark following behind looking quite smug. "Guess where he took me?" he challenged. "I don't know," I replied. There were so many places they could have gone to. "To Richard's," said Mark triumphantly. "You're joking!" I said, quite amazed. "Did he take you right to the door?" I asked. "Straight to the door and stood there waiting to go in," Mark said smiling. I asked Mark if he had knocked. "Yes, but Richard was out. Jack didn't want to leave, so I had to explain that Richard wasn't there, then we walked back up Green Ride and through the wood." I was quite astounded by Jack's perspicacity; he never ceased to amaze me.

Every so often, the restaurant would hold a special evening meal, sometimes accompanied by music, which could be shanty singers, jazz or baroque. On these nights, when on their walk, Jack would take Mark all round the car park, sniffing at all the cars, (Jack, not Mark). I should imagine Jack was probably saying to himself, "Hmmm, they've been here before. I recognise the smell." After inspecting all the vehicles, he would take Mark round all the trees in the rest of the car park and do whatever he had to do, Mark picking the poo up in a bag. The next thing to do was for Jack to take Mark to the gates of the stable yard and stand gazing through the windows into the brightly lit restaurant, at the diners enjoying their meal and music. If he had been allowed, Jack would have gone straight inside, said, "Hello everybody, what's going on here?" and inspected everyone and everything minutely. It wouldn't have looked too good with Mark swinging a bag of poo in his hand, so they stayed outside. Mark had to wait until Jack had had a good long look. When the music was indoors, the diners were unaware of Mark and Jack's presence. Occasionally, the music was outside and the restaurants tall French windows were flung open, so the diners could appreciate the music. This made Mark and Jack clearly visible, standing in the arched gateway, Jack, as far forward as he could get, watching and listening, tilting his head as he heard certain notes in the singing or playing. As far as the diners were concerned, the pair was probably a tramp and his dog, wondering if a few scraps of food might come their way.

When Jack was quite ready, they would return home, Mark often inadvertently bringing the bag of poo in. "No, I don't want that, thank you," I would tell him. "O.k. then, I'll put it in the bin," he would laugh. "Did Jack have a good look?" I would ask and Mark would relate what they had seen and heard, telling what had interested Jack the most and his enjoyment of it all.

CHAPTER 8

Hunting, Cheek and an Attack

Throughout the summer, Jack practised his squirrel and rabbit catching, trying to improve his techniques. Some squirrels he caught and killed without getting bitten. Squirrels seven, eight and nine, all bit him on his face or nose. He would squeal shrilly as the squirrel in his jaws turned and sank its chisel-like teeth into his lip. However hard it bit, he didn't let go. It seemed to anger him and shaking it madly, he would bite hard, killing it quickly, then bury it once it was dead. Jack was never concerned in the slightest about the bites on his face, although he wasn't too happy when his nose got bitten, which then gushed blood into his mouth. Salt water was used on his nose, as a dog's nose is very sensitive. After a while, it would stop bleeding but not before his drinking water was red and the kitchen walls splattered with red spots, when he shook his head to clear his nose.

Surprisingly, these wounds healed quickly and eventually left no sign of his battles with these rodents. By now, I'd come to realise it was no use trying to stop his strong hunting instincts. I had to accept Jack for who he was. Mark felt the same way too. We hoped he might calm down, though weren't too optimistic. It would be better if he learnt to catch and kill them without getting bitten. Normally, if anything hurt him, he didn't do it again, yet with squirrels, it seemed to have the opposite effect. At least the rabbits didn't bite him! They were usually dying anyway, because of myxomatosis; all Jack had to do was walk up to them, give them one bite, then bury. I wasn't too happy when he would come across a dead rabbit in the wood, which he would run of with and eat it. I would be sick with worry for a few days, until he proved to continue to be fit and well. I always feared they may have been poisoned.

These were the only two animals that Jack hunted, although I'm sure he would still think a stoat was some sort of squirrel. Luckily, stoats were far more secretive, so Jack never got the chance of finding out that they were different. Pheasants, partridges, ducks, geese and anything similar, he quickly learnt to ignore, which made life somewhat easier.

For some reason, right from the beginning, Jack had a thing about hedgehogs. Mark soon got to recognise when one was about on their evening walk, because of Jack's behaviour. It took Mark a long time to dissuade Jack from wanting to lunge at them. It's amazing just how fast a hedgehog can move when it wants to. I was out with Mark and Jack, when Jack went into hedgehog mode. "There's usually one in this area," indicated Mark to a patch of long grass. "There it is," he said as he shone his torch in that direction. Something shot out of the beam and into the shadows, Jack nearly taking Mark with him, as he too shot forward. "No," said Mark to Jack. The hedgehog was nowhere to be seen, as we searched the area, thinking that it couldn't really have gone that far. But it had. No matter how far we looked, it had certainly made itself very scarce. Well, I learnt something new that night. Maybe that's why Jack was interested; because they could make very sudden movements. It was in our garden that Jack finally learned to leave hedgehogs alone. They frequently visited our long grass areas after dark and so did Jack. He quite liked to mooch round in the dark and would ask to go out for this purpose.

He made this request before his walk one night, soon coming back to the door, asking to come in. As he seemed to be frothing at the mouth, I thought he'd been foolish enough to eat another toad. After eating a baby toad and finding it extremely distasteful, he ignored toads and frogs assiduously. Looking into his mouth, I thought his palette looked a little sore; he was salivating and licking the roof of his mouth a lot. When Mark and Jack were ready to go their walk, I told Mark, "Have a look round the garden with your torch. See if there are any hedgehogs about." Sure enough, a hedgehog was in the far corner of the garden, unharmed, very spiny and Jack didn't want to know. "They're not much fun. Let's go on our walk," he seemed to say, pulling in the opposite direction.

The next time Jack came across a hedgehog in our garden, he jumped towards it, hitting the grass near it with his front paws, barking and wagging his tail, telling it off for spoiling his fun, knowing that it would hurt his mouth to bite it. He left them alone after that!

On the first of July, the woods were declared open and once again, dog aromas filled every track, sending Jack's nose into transports of delight. Maybe this would take his mind off rabbits and squirrels. He was thrilled to meet his friends again, just as they were glad to be back in the woods, after weeks of walking on beach or cliff.

After questioning many dog owners on whether their dogs chased squirrels and rabbits, I was relieved to find that many did; so it wasn't just Jack. These included various terriers, spaniels, golden retrievers, Labradors, a Doberman, lurchers, dachshunds and a rough collie, some of which caught and killed them, and some eating them. It depended on some dogs having stronger hunting instincts than others. It wasn't just because Jack was a greyhound.

The Field Study Centre also made their return, bringing groups of school children to search the wood for 'monsters', who would leap out to drench them with Super-soakers. Jack avoided these groups as much as possible, due to him becoming entangled twice with the children, because he ignored my commands, thinking he knew best. He got the fright of his life when water showered down, with children squealing and screaming shrilly, around him. He ran a few yards and stood waiting for me. Forever after that, he always viewed children with suspicion, never being comfortable in their presence.

I knew most of the 'monsters' by sight and they knew Jack and I. If any still wore their grotesque and frightening masks, I would say, "Take your mask off quick, before Jack sees it. You'll frighten him to death," knowing how Jack would view it in detail, not understanding that it was a mask and become extremely fearful. I didn't want him to start to imagine frightening faces would be all over the wood and around every corner.

This year had been a bad one for ticks, probably due to higher numbers of deer, where we walked. I checked Jack daily and was thankful of the little tick removers, which made extraction easy, although some of the little blood-suckers got into very awkward places – between toes, on testicles, in that hollow on the outside of the front legs just at the wrist. Luckily Jack was so used to me doing things to him, he was very tolerant and a good patient, receiving much praise afterwards.

The only time fleas were visible, was just after Jack had caught a squirrel or rabbit. They didn't stay long, due to the insecticidal shampoo on Jack's fur, congregating on his ears before jumping off to die on the floor. I checked regularly for fleas or flea dirt but never found any. I changed his bedding frequently, just to be on the safe side. I did hear somewhere that fleas don't like black dogs, which sounds somewhat ridiculous but I did begin to wonder. Jim was predominantly white and I waged a running battle with fleas on him. Mind you, we did live in a town and the only fleas about were dog fleas, whereas here, the fleas are rabbit and squirrel, which apparently can't live on dogs, so I've been told.

With human and dog numbers increasing in the wood, the sightings of deer and their tracks diminished to their normal numbers and Jack's fear waned. I was successfully fighting my depression, gradually surfacing that deep sea and actually enjoying our walks through dappled shade, blue sky above and warm sunshine.

Everyone who knew Jack noticed straight away that he was no longer wearing his muzzle and I suspect the people whose dogs Jack teased, were quite worried by this change. However, time proved to them that Jack meant no harm, their worry ebbing slowly away.

In the middle of July, the plumber arrived during a torrential downpour that sent a river of water past our back door, two or three inches deep, which necessitated him coming to the front of the house before he could enter. He had come to start fitting the long-awaited central heating. After a brief hello, Jack took himself off to bed or any other spot where he normally lay, and slept while the work was carried out.

Two weeks later, the Rayburn was out and all the radiators and the boiler were in. Once the oil tank was in place, a trench had to be dug in our garden, to take the oil pipes from the tank to the house. Mark volunteered to do this, which the plumber was thankful for and a narrow trench was made along by the hedge, where Jack's racetrack was. Oh dear! I knew he wouldn't be pleased. We let him out and showed him the trench, so that he wouldn't suddenly run round and end up falling in the hole. The trench was inspected from end to end, along with the excavated soil, which ran along side like a small dyke. At the end by Jack's bushes, was a large mound of soil, which Jack cocked his leg on in disdain. Over the days prior to the pipes going in, Jack would run round the garden the best he could and end up scufting and scraping the large mound of soil, in an effort to get it out of his way. "No lovey," I would say to him, "It won't be here long, then you'll be able to run about as usual."

As soon as we got the go-ahead off the plumber, Mark and I filled in the trench and re-laid the turf, hoping that all Jack's running wouldn't tear the turf up again. When we showed him his racetrack was restored, after a careful inspection, a cheeky gleam came into his eye and off he shot round the garden, up and down, round and about, ending in the bushes for a good rend and dig. So that was all right then. And, the turf stayed in place.

The weather was pretty hot, so we didn't need to use the central heating, which was good. What wasn't so good was the fact that Jack got so hot in the sun or when it was warm weather. With him chasing squirrels, he would get alarmingly overheated, flinging himself down in any patch of long, cool grass for some relief and rest. I used to put his lead on for the rest of the walk, to prevent any more exertion on his part, as a greyhound can run itself into the ground if allowed, possibly with fatal consequences.

Although we had postponed our June holiday, we still had a week booked in North Wales for the first week in October and deemed it safe enough to go. As usual, rain fell as we travelled west, which cleared from the Midlands, to a beautiful afternoon run into Wales. This year I bought a sheepskin for myself, a Jacob, which Jack had a good poke with his nose, as it smelt of wool fat.

This year we had been able to rent a house in Borth-y-Gest, the small coastal village I'd known since childhood. The view from the front was across the harbour, to the hills on the far side of the estuary.

After unpacking, we walked into Porthmadog to buy chips, finding a bench overlooking the harbour to sit and eat, while Jack lay on the grass by our side. When we had finished, we walked back to Borth to find the sea coming in, slowly but surely, filling the harbour. A stream emptied into the harbour that mixed with the tide and in this confluence, we could just make out large fish swirling in the shallow waters – grey mullet. Jack was intrigued. Tilting his head to one side, pricking his ears even more than usual and insisting on watching for some time. Anything and everything was always of great interest to Jack, he seemed to want to experience as much as he could fit into his life.

As darkness crept up, we returned to the house, to have a hot drink before climbing the rather steep stairs, to bed. Jack rushed up with no trouble and sank into his new holiday bed. His old cardboard bed had started falling to pieces, which meant a replacement had to be found. Oval, thirty-seven inches at the widest point, a rich ruby red, soft yet with sides firm enough to lean his head on without it squashing to the floor. Covered with a wool blanket, lined with one of his sheepskins, his big cushion and his travel rug to tuck him in with, Jack was snug as a bug in a rug.

Early each morning, we walked round the headland, along the path above the small sandy coves, to the third beach, which was a long curve of sand. Jack thoroughly enjoyed all the dog smells and was delighted to scent and hunt the occasional rabbit, not that he caught any. Sometimes we would have the beach to ourselves and sometimes other dog walkers would be met with.

We were just descending the rocks at the far end, one morning, from a visit to Mum's 'grave', to find a group of people and dogs standing chatting nearby, on the beach. Jack stood half way down the rocks, considering things. One of the dogs was a black Lab bitch, which was standing facing the rocks in a slightly threatening manner. Jack knew that on the sloping rocks, he was vulnerable and he may not be able to out-manoeuvre the Lab if she chose to come forward. As he dithered, not being quite sure which course to take, I told him to come my way. I placed myself between the Lab and Jack, so he felt somewhat protected and he came down as quickly and as carefully as he could, dancing past the Lab, once on the damp sand.

As Mark and I walked up the beach, Jack must have decided to show the Lab that she would have had no chance anyway and also partly because he felt a bit silly for his worry, mixed with relief, he set off in a mad run from one end of the beach to the other, flying round and even dashing straight through the group of people and dogs, at the far end. All eyes were on Jack, including the black Lab. All conversation stopped while he flew round at top speed; we were all riveted. He looked fantastic and I'm sure he knew he had our attention. I did love him. I loved his cheekiness, his vulnerability, how he bravely faced his fears, his bravado and I loved his showing off, and last but not least, I loved to look at him; he was so handsome.

Another morning, we met a lady with a small terrier, which was off the lead. He was a game little dog and wasn't fazed by Jack trying to bar his way, trotting straight through Jack's legs. Jumping round Jack, he scampered about, making Jack dismiss his posturing to favour dashing about with his friend, even rushing into a choppy sea and having to swim out again. Jack just loved being with other dogs.

Susan, Malcolm and Leo paid a visit on one of the best days weather wise. A balmy day, warm and sunny. After a lunch, we walked to Morfa Bychan, Jack all the time encouraging Leo to follow him. On Morfa beach, which was vast, the tide had left many small, shallow pools between the gently undulating sand bars, looking like a hilly countryside peppered with lakes. Jack purposefully walked through each pool, while looking at Leo out of the corner of his eye, tail high in the air, a cheeky look on his face. Leo wasn't supposed to go in the water and nor did he like to but Jack wore him down. Susan wasn't pleased, as he followed Jack into each pool, Jack triumphantly leading the way with a self-satisfied look. He even looked as though he was smirking! I shook my head. "The things he gets up to," I thought. Although I couldn't help smiling.

On the way back, we had to traverse a steep, narrow track with a number of high steps, which slowed us humans down. I was always ahead, endeavouring to keep my eye on that cheeky Jack. His nimble feet and powerful muscles paid no heed to the steps we found so difficult. As I rounded a bend, puffing a bit, Jack was gone and so was Leo. Up we climbed until we came to a fork in the path. Our way was to the right and we had no way of knowing which way that cheeky monkey had taken Leo. Susan volunteered to go to the right calling for Leo, while Mark went left up an even steeper track. I had a feeling they could have gone left, as Jack loved to investigate everything new and had wanted to go up that track on a number of occasions, on previous days. I stood shouting, "Jack, Jack."

When Mark reached the top of the track, it opened onto a holiday park filled with brown, wooden chalets with little fenced verandas. Jack was just on his way back, with Leo following, as Mark appeared. "Come on, this way," said Mark. To avoid any capture, Jack skipped past Mark and shot off down the helter-skelter slope he had originally come up, to explode out in front of me, a cheeky gleam in his eye and flew off up the flight of steps, on the path Susan had taken, Leo chasing in his wake. Jack was extremely pleased with himself. He had not only found out where the track went but led an unsuspecting accomplice into a little bit of naughtiness too. Ah, this was the spice of life!

The next day saw us on Morfa Bychan again, when Carol and Eric visited. Us humans sat on a large piece of slate, to rest Carol's heart and my back. Jack wasn't interested in resting and busied himself pestering every dog which past or running round the headland on the beach, finding the boardwalk on the far side, then climbing over the headland to jump out behind us, just as we were wondering where he had gone. He enjoyed playing little jokes on us and liked to have little adventures. One thing was for certain; Jack could never be described as boring.

During our meal that evening, Jack behaved impeccably, with not even a nibble behind my back. By this time he was fully trustworthy with our food. I always instructed him quietly, not to touch anything and he would lay patiently, head on paws during the preparation and beside the table when we ate, waiting for his reward at the end of each course. He never stole any food ever again. He was a real treasure.

The evening prior to our departure, Mark vacuumed the house from top to bottom, while I got things together and did some cleaning. Jack stayed downstairs on his duvet, being more tolerant of the vacuum now. Later that night, when Jack and I had gone upstairs, me to do my teeth and Jack to climb into his bed, I heard a small noise from Jack. It was a cross between surprise and indignation. "What is it Jack?" I called. Silence. I carried on doing my teeth, knowing that something must have bothered Jack for him to make a comment out loud. When I finally went into the bedroom, it was very obvious what had upset Jack. There he was curled up, perched on top of his cushion in the middle of his bed, looking a little peeved. Every time Mark vacuumed, he moved things and didn't put them back again. He had left Jack's cushion inside the bed, instead of replacing it in the step-through. "Come on Jack, get up lovey. Let me move your cushion," I said, to a reluctant Jack. He was slow to respond yet once settled on his sheepskin and covered with his blanket, was far happier.

After a wet and windy start, our journey home brightened to a sunny afternoon. As we drove onto the estate, it was still light. "I'll tell you what," I said to Mark, "If you drop me and Jack off, we can walk back though the wood. It will do my back good and Jack will enjoy it." "O.k.," he replied, "Be careful."

Waving to Mark, I opened the gate to the wood and let Jack off. It was good to be back in our beloved woods with Jack trotting ahead of me, his small feet twinkling across the ground. I loved the way he seemed to flow along so noiselessly.

At home Mark unpacked the Land Rover and when Jack and I arrived, we found half the mulberry tree on the ground. Jack skirted round it carefully, avoiding any potential danger, while I went into the house and switched the central heating on. Mmm, utter luxury – no Rayburn to light. Instant warmth – lovely.

On Sunday, I helped Mark saw up the mulberry branches, while Jack chose to stay in the house. The weather had been strong winds and this continued for a few days more. Jack and I witnessed the top of a tree blow off, with such a crack that we both jumped. I used to tell him that if he heard a tree crack like that, to run if it was near him. Whether he understood, I'm not sure yet on very windy days, if we heard a tree crack nearby, Jack would run out of the way, then turn and wait. I too would run sometimes and always hurried through the Great Wood, where all the huge, ancient giants swayed in the gales.

Jack would wear his coat to keep cosy, while out on walks at this time of the year. His ear tips didn't look so cosy though. Despite the various steroid and anti-biotic creams, their condition had worsened to hair loss, flaking skin and swellings that burst open, leaking blood onto his duvet and on the wall by his water bowl. Because they bled, I decided to bathe them with Listerine, to prevent any infection. Jack seemed to find great relief in this, so I cut out the steroid and anti-biotic creams and just bathed his ears twice a day, with the Listerine.

Our vet organised for a homeopath to visit us, to try and find a more natural solution, as he was very reluctant to put Jack on steroid tablets, and so was I. By the end of October, when the homeopath visited, Jack's ears were already improving. However, to be on the safe side, he had causticum pills to take, and Bach Flower Remedy drops, in his water bowl. It was agreed that I carry on using the Listerine, as none of the ingredients would clash with the homeopathy.

Gradually, Jack's ear tips became less crusty and over time the skin appeared normal, with the hair growing back. When the homeopathic remedies ran out, I carried on with the Listerine, eventually cutting it down to rubbing Jack's ears once a day, as a preventative measure. His ears remained soft and velvety from then on, which was a good job as they caught the attention of the many people who admired him.

During November, on one of our walks, I was chatting to a lady who had stopped us, so she could admire Jack. He refused to say hello. Being and impatient dog and loathing standing about, he wandered off towards the cottage situated at the old exit of the property, which happened to be nearby. Next to this was a five bar field gate and an old wooden stile and also a dog-walker's track, worn into the vegetation up a slope and onto a lane. "Don't you go up there," I called to deaf ears. "No, Jack. Come here." Did he listen? Did he heck. "Ow, ow, ow," Jack shouted. "Oh no, now what's he done? I'll have to go," I told the lady, as I hurried in Jack's direction. Far from wanting to explore, Jack's little face now looked at me through the bars of the gate, with a, "Oh Mummy, I've hurt myself. Please help me," sort of look.

"Oh lovey. What have you done?" I asked him, as I walked up the worn path by the stile. "How on earth did you get there?" I said, as I observed a rusty strand of barbed wire hanging in the undergrowth, which I presumed he must have walked or jumped over. "Let me have a look at you," I said, crouching by his side. Everything seemed o.k. apart from a one inch hole, torn in the skin of his chest, just behind his right elbow. "Ah lovey. I'll make you better," I told him, giving him a hug, making him feel much happier. We then made our way straight home to treat the wound.

"Lie down," I instructed Jack, pointing at his duvet. He knew the routine and lay down with a sigh, so I could examine the wound properly. Dabbing it with Listerine, I expected him to wince. It mustn't have stung, as he never moved or made any comment. Shaking some Negasunt over the tear, I was glad it was well off the ground and didn't need a dressing, nor would Jack have to be kept on the lead for walks.

For the next three weeks, I checked the wound daily, wiping with Listerine and dusting with Negasunt. Jack couldn't reach it to lick it, so had to put up with it itching as it healed. I was quite surprised that the wound was fully healed by the end of the three weeks. Eventually the scar was lost in his hair and it was impossible to find where it had been.

Early December, after writing our Christmas cards out, I suggested to Mark that we walked down to Mary's to deliver hers and Rowans. Not being too keen, as he'd just come in from work, I managed to persuade him that it would do us all good and Jack would enjoy seeing his friends. He acquiesced.

It had been a beautiful afternoon, bright and sunny, so it was still quite light at three thirty p.m. when we set out. As we spotted Mary's car in the main car park, we knew she wasn't at home. We looked over towards the donkeys who were looking over the fence and hee-hawing, not having had their feed, so she wasn't there either.

"She must have taken Rowan towards the church," I said. "She might be in the church," Mark suggested. "Well let's go down there anyway," I said. Once in the church field we marched along the track, Jack putting his nose to the ground and beginning to hurry, dragging me excitedly towards the church. It was plain they'd come this way but were they at the church or had they walked past it and gone further?

As we approached the gate to the churchyard, Rowan appeared, to investigate the sound of our footfall, followed closely by Mary with a dustpan and brush in her hands. Going through the gate, Jack began displaying to Rowan, rather bouncily, nearly dragging me through the air. "Let him off," said Mary and I quickly followed her advice. Jack and Rowan bounded around whilst I helped Mary sweep the porch. Jack then took the opportunity of dashing past us into the church, then out again before I had time to say anything. "It's all right," Mary assured me, "Rowan goes in there too. They're all God's creatures."

When Mary went to put the brushes away, Rowan and Jack both rushed after her, with me on their tails. Jack was busy trying to see exactly what Mary was doing, then when she'd stowed the dustpan and brush, Jack turned and ran down the aisle, tail waving in the air, eyes bright, mouth laughing, gazing round in wonderment, while trying to take everything in. I called him and he ran back to me, desperately applying the brakes for a sharp left-hand turn on the stone-flagged floor.

Mary closed the door and once outside, Jack and Rowan went wild. Jack encouraging Rowan, he decided to disappear round the west end of the church, at a full run. We laughed. "I bet he'll run right round," I said. No sooner were the words out of my mouth, then Jack burst from round the east end, at great speed but instead of making for us, he flew straight through all the gravestones, to the opposite corner and after a tight bend, went for another lap.

Meanwhile, Rowan appeared rushing like a steam train, from the back of the church, looking disappointed at not seeing Jack. The next second, Jack flew past him and on across the churchyard, dodging gravestones. Rowan speeded up again to try and cut Jack off. Jack was too quick and after a short circle, he turned to bounce, growling excitedly in front of Rowan. We all laughed. They just looked so happy and were having so much fun it made us happy too.

As there were no sheep in the church field, we left them off their leads to continue their antics. Jack took the opportunity to pop along the fence line from the church to the car park, investigating interesting smells, which were probably rabbit-scented. With much encouragement from us, he came rushing back to show off to Rowan. What a lot of growling and bouncing about, although all in a ferment of good humour.

Too much mad running could strain a toe or tendons in a foot, which would result in some limping and occasional squeaks. As I checked his feet on a daily basis and knew each foot so well, I could spot any slight swelling quickly. Gentle massage and shortened walks on the lead, helped many of these strains to recover in three to six weeks.

A few days after the mad run round the churchyard, Mary and Rowan came to dinner. As they came down the garden, I opened the back door for Jack to go out to greet them. Rowan had other ideas. Heading straight for the open door, barged Jack and myself out of the way, to investigate the ground floor in great detail, leaving Jack to follow him round, a little put out by the intrusion without any greeting first.

Once satisfied, Rowan turned to make his addresses, enabling Jack to practice his dog etiquette. Mary was no trouble whatsoever! Rowan's blanket was laid on the floor and once both dogs were settled, we tucked into a steaming vegetable crumble, followed by fresh fruit jellies and banana cake.

Both dogs sat to attention before polishing off a small treat of the crumble each. With the dishes in the sink, we withdrew to the living room, where Jack climbed into his bed and Rowan lay a short distance away. I lit a log fire and we all relaxed, chatting to the accompaniment of the crackling of wood as it burst into flames. Rowan edged closer to Jack's bed and poked it with his nose, only to be warned by us and a rumble from the occupant, that that was Jack's realm only.

The following day, we were a little late surfacing but still went our normal walks. Being a Sunday, a few more people were about along with their dogs, as we walked up the woodland walk. Just before we could turn off onto a quieter track, a German shorthaired pointer male cantered up to where Jack was sniffing, looking very much like it was intent on a bit of bullying. Mark and I watched with interest, knowing that Jack was no pushover. As soon as Jack turned to see the dog, his body language spoke volumes and I think the bully quickly got the message, as his body language also changed, as if to say, "Oh no, I've got more than I bargained for here."

The bully moved off, Jack trotting by his side, just to drive home his point. Both dogs trotted to the bully's owners, then Jack left them to cock his leg. "Come on Jack," I called. Jack bunched up and started to run to me. Unfortunately, he had to pass between the bully and the undergrowth.

Hearing a sudden rush, the bully lunged sideways, cannoning into Jack who, taken by surprise, faltered in his stride and was knocked off his feet, ending up on his back in the brambles with the bully on top, going for his throat.

Mark and I tore down the path. All we could hear was snarling and growling. It looked a bit unfair to us. The bully's owners lashed their dog with his lead and pulled him off, just as we drew near. Jack jumped up and trotted out of the way, looking a little embarrassed at being taken advantage of in such an undignified manner. "Come here Jack, let me look at you," I called. Straight away he came to be examined and thankfully, I found no bites, although his leather collar had scrape marks from the other dog. As he also wore his Bio-flow, I think the two collars helped to protect his neck.

The bully, I noticed, had a very bloody nose, which I was pleased to point out to his owners. Good for you Jack! Jack only used his teeth when totally necessary and this episode certainly warranted their use. Further into the walk, I noticed a spot of blood on Jack's rear left foot and on closer inspection, found a puncture wound between two toes, caused by a sharp object. It was a good job he had been wearing his coat, as it surely protected his back against the spiny brambles.

His foot meant a bandage and lead-walking for two weeks, which was disappointing for Jack and for us, as Mark would be finishing for Christmas and our walks would not have the normal freedoms. At the end of December, the bandage was removed and Jack tried his foot out by racing round the garden in fresh snow. It was good to see him happy once more.

We did see that dog a couple more times, (once seen, never forgotten) and Jack had to be restrained from going after it. Not to attack it – that wasn't his style – but to posture round it and teach it some respect. It kept well out of his way anyway, probably not wishing for another bloody nose. After making enquiries, I found that although this dog wasn't a regular, it was local and apparently a 'blasted nuisance'.

CHAPTER 9

A Successful Summer

New Years day 2002, frost with a thick rime ice building, snow on the ground, cold and wintry, the woods looking immaculately clean, were peaceful and quiet. Taking full advantage of being on holiday, we roamed round the wood, coming across two roe deer, which bounded noiselessly off through the undergrowth. Jack coped well, showing no sign of panic. The only sign of any slight concern was his flicking ears, as he listened for evidence of one about to jump out on him.

As the weather remained cold, the snow stuck around for most of the week until the rain came to add to the slippery walking surface. Although Jack no longer careered wildly about, he still occasionally sustained an injury and as usual, it was on a weekend. The first Saturday in February, to be precise!

Because the woods were so muddy, Jack's legs, chest and inner thighs got spattered, necessitating a wash down on our return home. Shutting the kitchen doors to prevent escape, I half filled a small bucket with warm water, a little soap and a dash of Dettol, having a towel and a washcloth handy. "Right, come here Jack," I said, indicating the spot in front of me. Head down, not relishing the watery experience, he came to stand in front of me. The front feet and back feet on one side were rinsed, inspected and dried, Jack dutifully holding each foot up until I was finished. "Turn round," I told him and he walked up the room, turned round, then walked back to stand in front of me, only the other way round. I had achieved this originally, by holding his collar and leading him up the room, saying, "Turn round," as I turned him, then led him back into position ready to wash his other feet, for a period of days until he got the message.

While washing his other feet and undercarriage, I discovered a cut nearly three quarters of an inch long, along the side of the main pad of his front right foot. "Oh no. He's cut his foot. It's quite deep too!" I exclaimed to Mark, "It will probably need stitching. I'll phone the vet." After applying Listerine and Negasunt, along with a dressing, I spoke to our vet. "Is the blood soaking through the bandage?" he asked. "No," I replied. "We'll leave it until Monday," he said, making an appointment for Jack. It was a very clean cut and I couldn't work out what had caused it. Was it glass, metal or flint? Whatever it was, Jack had been unaware of it and didn't mind me ministering to his foot.

Some blood had soaked through the bandage by Sunday, so I re-cleaned and re-dressed the wound. Unfortunately, once again, we were back to lead walking and welly-boot wearing.

No breakfast for Jack and very early at the vets on Monday. After examining the cut, the vet decided not to stitch it. "It's very clean and doing well. Keep re-dressing every two or three days. It should heal all right. If you feel concerned anytime, just give me a ring," he told me. I bought a stock of dressings to use at home. Every two days, I wiped with Listerine and applied Negasunt, wrapping with fresh bandages. I must admit, I was amazed just how quickly it healed – in two and a half weeks. On the final day, when I decided Jack could go without a dressing, his poor little foot looked so squashed, (not that the dressing had been too tight – the hair was all flattened down), dry and fusty, that I thought I would give it a wash.

As he stood with his foot in the bucket of warm water, with a little soap and Dettol, the look on his face said it all, "Aah, that's wonderful." Showing no sign of wanting to remove his foot from the water, he stood for quite some time, enjoying the relief. I know how he felt. After having an operation, not having a bath for days, the stitches itching and muscles stiff, to sit in hot water was very welcome.

Even though fully healed, I kept Jack on the lead for a few days more. When he was let off, boy did he go off like a rocket. Greyhounds certainly revel in their ability to run at great speed and when deprived of that freedom, more than make up for it once liberty is restored.

During Jack's period of confinement to lead walking, work started re-designing the main visitor car park, which meant big machines, lots of earth moved, holes dug and it being closed off to cars. All this activity and changes were completely intriguing to Jack. Every day, when we were returning from our main walk, Jack had to stand looking into the car park through the wire fence, surveying all that was taking place, especially when a workman was digging a large hole. Standing inside, throwing the earth up onto a heap above him, the man toiled away. "He's digging a hole," I explained to Jack, "Come on lovey, you can come back tonight and have look with Daddy." I was quite sure Mark wouldn't mind – men like looking in holes don't they. Reluctantly, he took a few steps, then stopped again. I had to wait until he was ready to come along.

That night, Jack took Mark straight to the hole to make a thorough inspection. Every night, the whole car park and the days changes had to recorded and logged into Jack's brain and of course, a sprinkling of wee left on the big machines, to leave his mark. This went on for well over eight weeks and I'm sure Jack was pleased when it was all finished, all machines gone; just his car park back again, plus a few changes.

Part of our woods, namely the Deer Park, was out of bounds by March, as the bullocks had been put in sooner than expected. Jack missed going in the Deer Park and looked a bit fed up every time I said, "No, we can't go in there now, there are 'cows' in there." I always referred to all cattle as 'cows', when talking to Jack, so as not to confuse him. He seemed to know that I meant those big hefty things, which sometimes came after him.

Jack also got fed up with standing and waiting while Mark 'did' the donkeys for Mary, who had had an eye operation and mustn't get dust in her eyes. Two weekends, morning and evening, Mark fed and watered them, putting fresh bedding down too. Jack really took a dim view, ignoring the donkeys because it wasn't his choice to be there. It's not that he didn't like the donkeys – he did and they liked him too. On our walks, we quite often went to say hello to them, giving them a small bunch of grass each. On one occasion, as one of them put her head through the fence to take her grass, Jack poked her velvety nose with his pointy black one. "Excuse me!" she looked as though she was saying, as she pulled her head back. When she tried a second time, again Jack gave her nose a good poke, accompanied by a wagging of his tail. "Do you mind? I'm trying to eat my grass," she almost said, looking quite exasperated. Jack wagged his tail and smiled at me, as I asked, "Are you saying hello, then?" Third time lucky, as they say, as Mark handed the donkey her grass, unhindered. I'm convinced Jack was having a little joke with her, which she did not appreciate at the time, rather than just saying hello, as he could see that she was being given something to eat. Greyhounds usually have a cheeky sense of humour and Jack was no exception! In fact, he was the cheekiest greyhound I've known.

At Easter, it was lambing at the farm. Although Jack had never shown any interest in sheep, small lambs had attracted his attention, their weak bleating and shaky movements stimulating his hunting instincts. I always told him, "No," in a firm manner, as we walked through a field full of mothers and babies. This was done as frequently as possible to get Jack used to small lambs. He must have got the message eventually, as this year, when walking (on the lead), through the church field alive with gambling lambs, he nearly had a nose-to-nose encounter.

A gang of around eight lambs sprung about, chasing each other. Watching them as I walked, it was obvious they were intrigued by Jack in his red coat, as many animals proved to be. Our pace was even so as not to frighten the sheep and lambs. The gang just kept on coming, egging each other on. Jack knew they were coming to see him and I was pleased to see that his body language was showing a greeting – ears folded on head, head level, tail wagging level. Just before the lead lamb reached Jack, its courage failed and shying off to one side, all its friends following as it dashed off. Jack looked most hurt. Hugging him, I told him what a good boy he was, which seemed to cheer him up again.

A few days later, when ascending the steps up to the lawn, Jack's rear right foot slipped. Missing his footing, his knee smashed onto the edge of the concrete step. It sounded painful. Jack didn't cry out but carried on up to the lawn where he stood holding his leg up, not wanting to move it. Rushing out to have a look, there was only a small nick visible. Being right on a joint, I felt dubious and only rubbed his thigh to ease his pain. He tested his leg by walking round the garden and seemed happy with it. After dabbing it with Listerine, we went our walk, though shortened it somewhat.

Later in the day, the joint became very stiff and sore, making the act of lying down extremely difficult. I slept downstairs that night, on the settee, to look after Jack. Not that I got much sleep! I was up and down like a yo-yo helping Jack in and out of his bed. He couldn't quite lift his poorly leg high enough to clear the edge of his basket or cushions. Jack would put his front feet in, lift his bad leg as high as he was able, then I would kneel by him and gently lift the foot over the edge, to gently lower it into the bed, leaving him to do the rest. And vice versa to help him out. He just could not settle.

The next morning, after a very short walk and his breakfast, Jack managed to lie on his duvet. As I tried to apply ointment to his prepuce, I accidentally touched his bad leg. Like lightening, Jack's teeth hit my skull accompanied by a very annoyed yelping-snarl. "Don't you bite me," I said sternly, feeling hurt. Jack got up and left the room to stand about, unable to lie down again, looking totally miserable.

Trying to ignore him, I sat and wept into my breakfast, feeling horrible. Why couldn't I have just left him lying on his duvet and not bothered with his ointment for his prepuce? Mark put his arm around me, which made me feel even more guilty. "I've hurt Jack and now he can't lie down," I sobbed. Full of remorse, I got up and went to find Jack. Putting my arms around him, I told him how truly sorry I was, tears falling onto his fur, as I kissed his head. I wondered if he felt bad about biting me, since he was very eager to patch things up. Although I could see he forgave me, my guilt remained, as I couldn't take back what I'd done.

After finishing my breakfast and making sandwiches and salad for lunch, Jack was still standing in the same position. He had been there for one hour. My heart bled for him. "Come on lovey, you must lie down," I entreated as I went into the living room and patted the sheepskin in his bed. Jack followed me. "I'll help you. Come on, lie down in your bed," I said. He put his front feet in and I helped his poorly leg. Once in bed, he turned this way and that, not being able to find a comfortable way of actually lying down. He wanted to step out, so I helped him. Again I implored him to get back in. After much to-ing and fro-ing, Jack finally managed to lower himself down onto his sheepskin, with his head on his cushions. Carefully laying his travel rug over him, I breathed a sigh of relief, hoping that he would stay there.

I telephoned the vet for some Rimadyl to ease the pain and reduce any inflammation, which would have to be picked up later that day. Meanwhile, I put the television on and sat watching the Queen Mother's funeral, not daring to move for fear of disturbing Jack, who lay in the same position for five hours solid.

When Mark came in for lunch, Jack surprised me by leaping out of his bed, moving far more easily. Well, I suppose he was ready for his share of our sandwiches! After lunch, Jack and I went for a short walk, on the lead. On our return home, he was able to lie down a little easier. Even so, I still gave him a short course of Rimadyl tablets.

The following day the leg continued to improve, with Jack scampering up and down the garden steps and being able to lie in any position. He did pay a lot of attention to the wound, licking it at every opportunity. It looked as though the bone had been chipped, so it must have been excruciatingly painful at first. Although I kept my eye on it, occasionally dabbing with Listerine, I let Jack look after this one.

A few days later, Jack stepped on a sharp splinter of wood, which had been left by the wood yard, after they had cleared a fallen tree. Luckily it didn't puncture the foot but just left a graze between the pads. If there is anything sharp around, you can almost guarantee a greyhound will step on it. Please let this be the end of the accidents and please let him have a good stretch without wounds or bandages.

One of Jack's nipples on his abdomen had always been a little bigger than all his others. Suddenly, it became quite swollen. The vet checked him all over, including his testicles, instructing me to keep my eye on it. It measured 5mm across at times, changing from black to mottled pink yet never got any larger and most times growing smaller again. Occasionally it must have itched, as Jack licked and nibbled it, so I wiped it with Listerine, which he seemed to appreciate, indicating some degree of relief. While this nipple concerned me and I kept a close eye on it, it never came to anything.

Near the end of May, Jack and I were wandering along on our usual main walk towards home, when I stopped to wait, due to him lagging behind for a really good sniff. The sun was out at this moment, making it warm and relaxing. Hearing a rustling and wondering what it was, I glanced up to see two grey squirrels chasing about in a tree. They both came down onto the ground, oblivious of me. I glanced towards Jack as he trotted to me, quite unaware of the goings on. He stood on the path, facing me. Once on the ground, the squirrels parted company, one going to my right into the undergrowth. The other, still seemingly ignorant of both Jack's and my presence, came straight towards us and ran into Jack's feet, as he stood there in disbelief.

Not being one to pass up on an opportunity like this, he quickly bent down to grab the squirrel in his jaws. Albeit he'd grasped the squirrel round the chest and was squeezing, it turned and sank its incisors into Jack's nostril. Jack gave one yelp and spat the squirrel out, which landed with a loud thud on the track, then crawled through the fence to die. I suspect this bite hurt more than previous bites, due to the fact that Jack had not chased and no adrenalin was pumping round his body.

After a hug, we walked home as quickly as possible, leaving a trail of blood drips along our path. By the time we reached the house, the blood was not dripping so much. I bathed Jack's nose gently with salt water and was able to see that the squirrel had cut a nick, nearly a quarter of an inch long, into the top right side of the nostril, on the flap which opens and closes when scenting things. Oh dear. I hoped this wouldn't leave a slit when healed.

Once again, blood spread through Jack's drinking water, up the walls, on his duvet, on carpets and in his biscuit bowl. For a couple of days more, blood did leak out as Jack pushed his nose into his biscuit bowl but after a week, the cut had closed and healed, leaving a pink scar. In time, this too disappeared, as the pink turned to black and not even a dint remained.

June arrived and so did our postponed holiday in the Cotswolds. What a fabulous, sunny, hot day, too hot for travelling really, especially for Jack. Our destination was the quiet village of Naunton, not far from Stow-on-the-Wold. The accommodation, a barn conversion next to the owner's house. A lot of the work had been done by the owner, including the staircase, which was in three short sections, with wide, shallow steps making it very easy for Jack to walk up.

After settling in and eating our tea, we went for an exploratory walk, up one of the lanes out of the village and across the fields. We were delighted to find a myriad of wild flowers and birds, as we followed signposts over the hill, until eventually wending our way down various dusty tracks, Jack stopping to stand in puddles to cool his feet, we reached a road. "We'd better go back now," I suggested, as Jack and I were tired. Returning to our base, we had an early night.

BANG, BANG, BANG. I woke suddenly. What was someone shooting at this time of the night for? BANG, BANG, BANG. Pop, pop, pop. Jack shot out of his bed and was prevented from descending the stairs by a child-gate. "Fireworks," said Mark. Jack, panicking, rushed to and fro, then crammed himself between Mark's bed and the wall, going as far as he could, short of climbing up the other wall. As I put the light on, Mark got up and struggled to get Jack to reverse back into the room, put him in his bed, then settled him down. Although we heard a few more, Jack stayed put as I assured him it was, "All right," and that, "We are here."

The next day, on enquiry, we discovered that an operatic concert had been held, as part of the Queen's Jubilee celebrations and the firework display came at the end. No more were going to be let off that week. Good, I was glad about that.

Cirencester was down for a visit that day, owing to my wish to reacquaint myself with the town that I had stayed near, numerous times during my camping years. Another hot day for the drive and not all enjoyable. Half way there we could hear an unusual sound emanating from under the bonnet of the Land Rover. Just managing to reach Cirencester, we parked in the first car park we came across, then stared under the bonnet, poking and pointing.

"Let's walk into town and ask if there are any Land Rover enthusiast garages round here," I suggested. After offering Jack a drink of water, we hurried through the streets. On meeting a policeman, I asked him. He didn't know, he wasn't from around here. Looking out for other Land Rovers, I thought it would be more fruitful asking the owners. Very quickly, I spotted one pulling up. O.k. the man looked a bit, well, different but dismissing this, I made my enquiry. It turned out he actually lived in Wales, having come back to Cirencester for a while. He didn't seem to know what the problem was, from my description of the symptoms, talked a lot, often repeating himself, saying he would meet us at the Land Rover in half an hour – 'he just had to buy some beer first'. His breath was already laden with alcoholic fumes. I wished I'd never asked him. "Did you notice he wasn't wearing any underpants?" said Mark, referring to the man's black, slightly Nora Batty leggings, ending in big boots and being quite lumpy round the block and tackle region. "Yes," I said, wishing even more that I'd never clapped eyes on him.

Resignedly, we trailed back to the car park to meet the man by the Land Rover. Jack patiently waiting while we all hung over the engine. On the chaps' instruction, Mark fired her up. Leaning in, intently listening, I really feared the man's long, dark unkempt locks were just about to be caught up in the large fan and belts, spinning at a great rate of knots, millimetres from his hair. It soon became clear no matter how helpful he wanted to be, he wasn't much actual help. Mark gave me the card with the breakdown recovery/repair number on, which we'd never used before. The man still repeated himself, even more so now and didn't seem to want to go, looking a bit upset that I was going to phone the breakdown firm. Thankfully, he drove off as I was in the conveniently situated phone box, in the car park. While we waited for them to arrive, we walked Jack up and down in the shade, giving him another drink.

At last the breakdown van turned up and we were told that the alternator was loose. A few turns of a spanner and feeling at ease, we walked back into town to have a look round. I didn't recognise a thing. My perception after all those years was totally different. Never mind. We wandered round looking for Black Jack Street, so I could take a photo of Jack by the sign, which turned out to be disappointingly high up but I took one nevertheless; looked at the architecture, then wandered back through a park.

Hot and tired, we drove back the way we had come. Unfortunately, we soon heard a familiar noise under the bonnet. Feeling a bit stressed, we limped back to base, the noise gaining in volume the closer we got. Once again, I rang the breakdown service and two hours later, a different chap arrived to tell us we needed a new alternator but he wouldn't be able to get one and fit it until Wednesday, due to the Bank Holidays.

The owners of the barn were very sympathetic, kindly offering us the use of one of their cars, which we took them up on the following day, to go to the nearest supermarket in Stow. Jack, being used to the back of the Land Rover, didn't cope well with the back seat of a car. I laid a towel along the seat, let Jack climb in, then I joined him, which he thought was novel and rather good – until we started to move!

The journey was probably around four miles, although this was long enough. Jack stood on me, sat on me, leaned on me, nearly fell off the seat numerous times and totally squashed me. Mark went into the supermarket, while Jack stood on me to put his head out of the window, as we waited. The journey back was equally as fraught, as Jack, instead of standing or sitting leaning against the seat back, insisted on leaning forward, stepping into thin air every now and again, each time we cornered. It didn't do my back any good, struggling to keep him on the seat. It was a great relief to get back to the barn and get out of the car. Jack was quite bemused by it all, looking as if to say, "The things they put me through." "There's no way we're using the car again," I said emphatically.

For the rest of the day and the following two days, we walked all round the immediate area, which was a bonus really. Quiet and relaxing, lovely countryside all around, filled with some different birdsong than we got at home. We had been told of badger sets and were surprised to find one of their entrances directly onto a road; a huge mound of sandy earth, quite obviously well used. Jack took one sniff and nearly dragged me up the road in the opposite direction. Maybe the strong mustelid scent reminded him of deer. Whatever, he didn't want anything to do with badgers.

Horses were everywhere. Everyone rode them and every hedgerow sheltered them. Racehorses abounded. Beautiful and graceful, we were attracted to a group of eighteen in a field we were passing. As the weather was cooler with a possibility of rain, Jack wore his little red raincoat. The horses crowded against the rather worryingly low fence, jostling each other to get a good look at Jack. Refusing to go near, Jack stood in the road looking into the distance. I could tell he was concerned, although he wasn't making it obvious. The horses seemed convinced he was a small horse, what with his pointy ears and red coat. Surely, he must be. Nipping and kicking each other, they were becoming increasingly boisterous as they fought to get to the front, nearest to Jack.

"Let's go," I said and we walked as calmly as we could, down the narrow lane, hoping that the horses wouldn't jump their fence and come after us. Back in the village, we felt safe although Jack still attracted attention but from men, who commented out loud on his good looks. We found this wherever we went, usually men or lads would have to stop and stroke him admiringly or couples or groups of people would stop and stare, wondering 'what is he?' I have never had a dog who was so admired by strangers. Visitors to the estate at home would sometimes approach asking, "Is this Jack?" and when I answered in the affirmative, they would say, "We thought it was. We met you last year. We were just saying we wondered if we'd meet Jack again." I was quite stunned by this. It was evident he made a big impression on many people. Not that Mark and I took him for granted; we revered him. We knew how special he was.

Wednesday came round and so did the new alternator, along with rain, rain, rain. After another trip to the supermarket, we visited a few villages with nice sounding names. Some were lovely but some exceedingly disappointing due to commercialism. On one of these trips, as we passed a woodland, I commented that it would be a good place to walk Jack, assuming that it was private and that we wouldn't be allowed in. Reaching a road junction, we turned left and saw a National Trust sign. "It's National Trust!" I exclaimed, "Shall we go back and have a walk?" "Good idea," replied Mark, "Jack could do with one."

The car park had two other vehicles and some restored barns. No one was about. Following a designated circular route, we soon entered the wood. Knowing that it was fenced in, we let Jack off. After days of lead walking, he dashed off, disappearing round the bend in the track. Presuming he was going to explore and not wait for us, we called out, "Jack, Jack," and ran after him. Just as we reached the bend, Jack came flying along, shooting past us going in the opposite direction. I burst out laughing, as he turned and galloped to us, smiling and waving his tail in the air.

The walk carried on through the wood, crossed the end of a cricket pitch, through more trees, round the perimeter of fields, then back onto the driveway to the car park. Jack was wonderfully behaved, not wandering too far and coming when called. Ahead of us at the conclusion of the walk, even though we approached the car park from a different direction, Jack knew exactly where it was and went straight to the Land Rover. After giving Jack a hug and much praise for being so good, we put him in the Land Rover, where he lay down with a, "I enjoyed that, thank you," sort of look.

Friday, we stayed at base, just going local walks in the rain. Saturday, we travelled home bathed in sunshine. That night, after saying, "Night, night," to Jack, as we opened the dining room door to the stairs, he hurtled past us and dashed up to the bedroom. "That's unusual," we said to each other. Every time we came home from holiday where Jack slept upstairs, he always went back to sleeping downstairs once at home again.

"O.k." I said to Jack, "You can sleep up here but you'll have to sleep on the carpet." He didn't care. As long as he was with us, he was happy. It took me a while to work out why he was so insistent on sleeping upstairs. Every night from then on, he came up with us. Fireworks in Naunton. That was it. He didn't want that to happen while he was alone downstairs, so he made sure he had us to protect him.

Another thing he brought back from Naunton was a sedate and stately walk up the stairs. No bounding – just walking. Occasionally, at the foot of the stairs, he would hesitate, thinking too hard about it, not being able to remember which foot went first. His front feet would start on the lower stairs, then he would bring them down again. Up, down. Up, down. Waiting with him, I would offer helpful advice like, "Don't think about it too much. Just pretend you're going up the garden steps." Once all four feet were padding upwards, he was fine. I would follow behind to make sure he was all right. Another thing he changed was that he ascended on the right, keeping the wall on his right although he still descended on the left, still keeping a wall on his right.

Sometimes Jack would lie by Mark's side of the bed yet it was apparent, due to his restlessness and waking me, that he would be more comfortable in his holiday bed. I relented. Bringing his holiday bed out of storage, I covered it with a wool blanket and placed a cushion in the step-through. Jack thought that was much better. Mark and I got used to having Jack in the bedroom at night and on the very odd occasion he decided to sleep downstairs, we really missed him.

Jack would quite often want to go up to his holiday bed, or upstairs bed, during the day, so I would leave the dining room door open. Having to go in the garden one day, I knew when I picked up the keys that Jack would hear me. And he did. Hearing his feet on the landing, I called out, "I'm only going in the garden." Surprisingly, Jack stayed where he was. Once in the garden, I looked up. There he was looking at me through the landing window.

Vice versa, Jack was in the garden one day with Mark, while I happened to be upstairs on the landing. Seeing Jack, I just could not resist opening the window and calling out, "Hello Jack. Hello Little Jack." He grinned and waved his tail. The next minute he scampered down the steps and into the house. Laughing to myself as I closed the window, I presumed he was being a silly Billy and had just run into the kitchen. Looking out of the window, expecting to see him shoot out into the garden again, I was taken by surprise as he dashed up the stairs, looking very pleased with a, "Here I am Mummy!" look on his face. Laughing even more, I put my arms around him to give him a big hug. "Hello Little Jack. What a clever boy you are," I told him.

Taking Jack to a large antiques fair held at a racecourse in Newmarket, we encountered a sweeping granite staircase in the members enclosure. Jack took it all in his stride, elegantly gliding up the steps by our side. Nor was he fazed by the packed crowds of people, many of whom admired him. Reaching a long window, which was from floor to ceiling, Jack stepped back quickly, thinking he was about to step off the edge. Peering out at the people below, ears erect, Jack tilted his head from side to side, trying to make sense of what he saw.

Jack enjoyed being able to come with us, looking at all the stalls, going into all the buildings and meeting many people. However, this was not quite the same as a walk in the woods, being extremely tiring. He was glad to jump into the Land Rover for a good rest. On reaching home, we all went for a quiet walk in the woods, to calm ourselves down after the crowds.

One of the few jobs I could still do was ironing, as long as it wasn't for too long. When I did my ironing, the end of the ironing board pointed towards Jack's big bed. Jack would usually be comfortably ensconced, while I prepared to iron. Because of the hard water in the region, my iron had soon refused to allow any water to be sprayed from a nozzle on the front. So for extra dampening, I resorted to a plant spray containing cold water, which did the job admirably.

As I busily ironed, watching television and running over my hand every now and again with the hot iron, I used to wonder why Jack would look at me, give a, "Hmph," then climb out of his bed and retire to the far end of the room. As I sprayed one day, I noticed that the fine mist was going further than I had imagined; all over the end of the coffee table. It was then that I realised why Jack kept removing himself from his comfortable bed, when I ironed. Plainly, he did not appreciate a fine drizzle falling on him whilst trying to sleep! In future I would angle the spray away from Jack and if I ever forgot, I would apologise profusely, whereupon he would briefly open a beady eye, as if to say, "Just be more careful, if you don't mind," before tucking his nose under a cushion.

Although Jack would paddle in water to cool his feet, this was of his own choosing. He wasn't too welcoming of unsolicited attention of the watery kind. I never used water as a deterrent, as some people do, as I did not wish Jack to view water as a punishment. In all the documentaries I have watched about wolves, I never witnessed the pack leaders using plant sprays filled with water, to stop another pack-member from carrying out an unwanted action. They normally used vocal commands and so did I.

Still, the plant spray was used as a method of cooling Jack down in hot weather. At first, he viewed this with some loathing. I always used the same words, "Let me spray you to cool you down." Eventually Jack, finding that the dampness rubbed into his fur, gave him considerable relief on hot days, actually welcomed the spray, coming forward readily to patiently stand and receive his shower. This was carried out prior to and after walks, when necessary.

Each spring around April or when the temperature outside was high enough, I would give Jack a bath in the garden, to strip out all the loose winter coat, following up with another a month later. Four buckets full of warm water would be placed in a curve by the mulberry tree. A jug, shampoo, facecloth, towel and water-brush were put easily to hand. On went an old T-shirt, leggings and Wellingtons. Hair tied back, I would fetch a lunging rein, which I would loop around Jack's neck like a noose, then lead him out to the tree. He knew what to expect.

Tied to the tree with no escape, Jack endured the water and shampoo with

17　Jack about to wee on corner post in disgust

18　Jack being carried down rocks near Garreg Goch

19   Running, after his unplanned swim

20   Jack in snow; cheeky attitude

21   A meeting with Mary and Rowan

22   "You'll never catch me"

23 "Phew, I didn't half enjoy that run

24 "Where's that squirrel?"

25   Jack
sitting (of his
own accord), by
his bushes

26   Jack
in the manner
of Anubis

27   Jack with Mark in Black Jack Street, Cirencester

28   Jack and Mark on a walk over the hill

29   A good bit of kicking never goes amiss

30   Worried Jack because Mummy is outside the Land Rover

31 Jack and me up Snowden- "We're not going all the way up there are we?"

32 "I want to go down now Mummy"

some stoicism. The facecloth was used to cover his eyes when I poured water over his head. He hated that, shaking water out of his ears and moving a little further away every now and again, threatening to garrotte himself, necessitating me having to push him nearer the tree and loosening his 'noose'. Once lathered up, I used the water brush, especially on his back, to pull out the loose fur. After a good dowsing to rinse all the shampoo away, I would rub Jack briskly with his towel.

The first time I bathed Jack in the garden, I made the mistake of letting him go after the towelling down. Instead of saying, "Look how clean I am Mummy," he ran madly round the garden, jumping in his bushes for a vigorous bout of digging, sending clouds of dusty soil and desiccated conifer bursting into the air. When Jack finally emerged, tongue lolling and a definite air of triumph surrounding him, he was coated in soil. As he was still damp, there was no point in trying to brush the soil off. I guessed that once Jack had dried out, the grit would fall off the smooth, shiny fur. And, thank goodness it did just that. Ever after, I always kept the lunging rein on until we were back in the house, where Jack once free, could then wipe his head on his duvet and anything else that he deemed suitable!

Susan, Malcolm and Leo came to visit near the end of June. Malcolm, constantly tired due to hard work, fell asleep on the settee. Susan, Mark and I were in the kitchen, chatting and watching the birds through the window, when Jack quietly appeared and made it plain he wanted to go into the garden. "He's after squirrels," I told Susan, "It's amazing to see how he creeps up the steps, then stalks them in the long grass." "Don't let Leo out then, he'll spoil it by running onto the lawn and chasing them," Susan said. As silently as possible, I let Jack out. "He won't get any," I said, "He just enjoys it." Susan was impressed by the way Jack kept as low as he could, as he ascended the steps, then stalked painstakingly round the edge of the long grass, stopping stock-still if he thought he'd been spotted. As far as we could see, there weren't any squirrels there. Jack carried on inching round, concentration at optimum. "There must be one there," I said a split second before Jack charged like a leopard, picked up a squirrel, shook it madly, squeezing it hard, then walked out of the long grass in his own little satisfied world. "Good grief!" I said, "Would you believe that!" Susan was even more impressed, calling to Malcolm that Jack had just got a squirrel. Malcolm entered the kitchen just in time to see Jack trot down the steps with his squirrel, to bury it in the compost heap.

That was a Sunday. The rest of the week, Jack did the same thing every day, catching and killing a squirrel each time. Apart from Wednesday that is, when he caught nothing. Making up for it on Thursday, when on our way home from our main walk, he must have seen his chance because he dashed across a grassy ride, into the trees on the far side and came out with a squirrel, which he killed and buried. Ten minutes later, as we entered our garden, he got another in our long grass. All this squirrel catching was enough to make me dizzy. By the end of the week he had caught seven. His total tally overall, was twenty. This earned him the name of Squirrel Jack. Due to the long grass area becoming totally squashed flat, this squirrel catching frenzy came to an end, as they could spot Jack coming. Even though he'd got seven in one week, six of those in our garden, squirrel numbers did not diminish, unfortunately.

Although Jack wasn't catching squirrels, he did take us unawares with a rabbit in the woods, early on another Sunday morning. A few yards ahead, as Mark and I were chatting, in a flourish Jack pounced, then ran off with a large rabbit in his jaws. "Did you see him get that?" I asked Mark. "No, I wasn't looking that way," he replied. We hurried after Jack, wondering if the rabbit was already dead before Jack came along or if it had myxomatosis. He was at the top of the slope waiting. Mark wanted to take the rabbit off him but Jack had other ideas, starting to gallop further into the wood and not in the direction he should have been going. "Jack," I called, at the same time saying to Mark, "If we chase him, we'll never get it. Let's carry on our walk and let him carry it." Mark agreed. It worked. Jack came back but instead of carrying on the walk, he lay just off the path and started to eat his rabbit. "Oh, this is all we need," I said, "Just when we're in a hurry too." We had planned to go to look at another antiques fair locally, after breakfast. Mark and I sat on a large, fallen bough to wait. "I hope no one comes along," I remarked, as we could hear a loud crunching of bones.

With half the rabbit eaten Jack got up and carrying the rest, came along with us. At last! But no, he seemed to want to find a burying place. In and out of the trees he padded. No this isn't good enough; someone might find it here. No, that's no good either. "Oh flipping heck. I wish he'd make his mind up," I groaned.

Dissatisfied with every possible hiding place, Jack half lay, bottom in the air, in the path and set to again, eating the rest of his rabbit. By the time he was fit to burst, one leg remained, which he put in the undergrowth. Needless to say, when he got home, I did not open a tin of meat for him!

After a quick breakfast, Mark and I went out to our fair, for a browse round, returning a couple of hours later. After greeting Jack in the kitchen, which was always with us kneeling down hugging him for some minutes, Mark walked into the living room. "What's this on the floor? Come and have a look," he told me. Switching on the light, I scrutinised a large spherical bodge. "It looks like it's half of that rabbit. It was obviously too much for him," I said philosophically, going to fetch my washing up gloves and newspaper to wrap the rabbit remains in, throwing them in the bin, (outside!), and wiping the carpet of any remnants. I didn't say anything to Jack; it was just one of those things.

Some days later, on our very early morning walk, Jack and I had gone down to the churchyard, which was one of his favourite places due to the vast numbers of rabbits that populated the area. Once through the gate, I let him off so he was free to follow scents, while I wandered round. Very quickly, he put up a rabbit, which had been hiding in the long grass. Being still near the gate and not wanting Jack to be disappointed if it got away yet also becoming increasingly drawn into his world by his zest and enthusiasm, I jumped in front of the rabbit as it ran for the gate. It turned, running back towards Jack, then turning again, it ran my way. It was impossible not to get involved and to try to help him, so I ran to cut it off, managing to turn it once again towards Jack, then it turned again quickly and leapt for the gate. I couldn't do any more; I was fagged out, useless; so slow and clumsy. Jack was on its tail. The rabbit misjudged the jump, momentarily hitting one of the bars of the gate. That was all Jack needed, that one mistake. He snapped it up and killed it. Strangely enough, although he welcomed my help in catching it, he did not want to share it with me and ran off to bury it in the corner of the churchyard.

He didn't seem to want to leave it either and when I went to get him, he grabbed for his rabbit and was about to run off. "Look lovey, I don't want your rabbit. Let me put your lead on and you can take it home with you," I explained to him. I don't know if he understood but he allowed me to fasten his lead to his collar.

All the way home, he carried his rabbit proudly, tail held high and as far in front of me as his lead would allow. In the garden, I let him off and he buried his prize in the compost heap, then came in wanting his breakfast, however, not before going to tell Daddy about him catching a rabbit.

Every evening, Jack insisted that Mark take him to the churchyard and the field at the back. Mark reported great numbers of rabbits sitting out on the grass and how Jack had chased them. I accompanied them one evening and indeed there were vast numbers of rabbits. To see Jack flying after one he'd chosen was incredible. Not that he caught any. The only time that would happen was if the rabbit made a mistake.

Mark too became influenced by Jack's sheer determination in doing what he loved best and took him around the church area. If Jack came back limping, due to an old racing injury, which made him go lame after running hard, I would remonstrate with Mark, telling him to keep Jack on the lead. I would massage Jack's shoulder and Mark would resist the temptation to let Jack off – only until Jack had recovered from his lameness, that is.

One night in early August, Mark opened the back door on the return from his walk with Jack. "Look in the garden," he instructed me rather proudly. Gazing out, my eyes fell on Jack, sitting on the lawn, jaws tightly clamped round a very large rabbit. "Good grief, that's huge!" I exclaimed, "How on earth did he get that. Did it have myxy?" "No. He got it all by himself and it's healthy," Mark's words tumbled out in excitement as he related Jack's triumph. "You should have seen him. He cut it off at the fence. He's worked out that they always run to the fence and he ran between the rabbits and the fence. He got this one just before it reached the wire."

I couldn't help feeling proud also. Jack was like our baby. There was no way we could pour cold water on his successes with rabbits and squirrels. I had observed the differences in Jack's body language when he had been successful in catching his quarry and when he had failed. When successful, his confidence shone; he was relaxed and satisfied. When outwitted by his quarry, he was quiet, looking disappointed and down, usually wanting to visit every rabbit warren in the surrounding area, to try again. This was not granted, especially if he had run hard. I used to tell him it didn't matter; he didn't have to catch them and not to take it so seriously. But, that was Jack – a perfectionist, just like me.

The huge rabbit, which looked pregnant, was duly deposited in the compost heap and covered over for the night. The next morning, a couple of hours after his breakfast, Jack dug up his rabbit, took it up on the lawn and proceeded to eat it. As our garden stretches past our next-door neighbour's kitchen, I sincerely hoped that Betty, our elderly neighbour, was not looking out of her window. Although I couldn't hear the crunching of bones from inside the house, I could see Jack pulling out the intestines, like green spaghetti, stretching his head into the air in an effort to snap it.

This was a scene we got used to. Well, mostly me, as Mark was usually at work. Jack ate a good portion of his rabbit before re-burying it. Rabbit, fur, bones and everything clearly takes a lot longer to digest that a tin of meat. Jack remained fat and stuffed all day, plodding sedately on his afternoon walk.

The rest of his rabbit was retrieved once again, on the following day, covered in decaying grass clippings and soil, to be consumed in full view of the window, by Jack, who looked very fulfilled and satisfied with life. When discussing Jack's propensity for rabbit eating with the vet, it was decided the best thing would be to worm Jack on a regular basis.

One time when Jack was after a rabbit, he impressed me no end by his quick thinking. We had just entered the Deer Park, Jack going ahead and to my left, into a small 'valley', when he surprised a rabbit that had been sitting in the open. Back and to they darted until the rabbit dived into a bramble patch. Each time it tried to make a run for it, Jack cut it off, just missing picking it up. Deciding to take a chance, the rabbit shot out and made for the fence along the back of the Deer Park. Instead of chasing it, Jack dashed past me and round to the gate, which we had just come through, hoping to find the rabbit on the other side. Dancing up and down, glancing over at me as if to say, "Stop wasting time Mummy, come and open the gate," Jack looked at me as though I was an imbecile. "No lovey, there's no point. It's gone now. Come on, it's gone. You can't get round there, there are too many brambles," I called out. After a while, Jack did come with me but I felt so guilty as we crossed the Deer Park – I should have let him out so he could have found out for himself that he couldn't have got through the brambles. I did apologise to him later.

I was glad Jack did not show the same interest in sheep. The lambs were now quite stocky and well grown. Nevertheless, they could still get up to mischief. On our six thirty a.m. Saturday morning walk, as we neared a bend in the woodland track at the back of the farm, Jack being a few feet ahead, two sturdy lambs trotted round the corner to face us. I only had time to say, "Oh!" before, seeing Jack, eyes starting from their heads, the lambs turned tail and galloped off as fast as they could.

"No," I said quietly to Jack, just in case he had other ideas. He looked as surprised as we were by their arrival and their swift departure yet paid no more attention than that; resuming his inhaling of dog scents, amongst other things more interesting. Although we could clearly observe their tracks heading towards the dog-walker's car park, they made no more appearances in the wood. Their great escape was related to the farmer on our return home. I wonder if coming face to face with Black Jack, made them reform their errant ways!

CHAPTER 10

Stings and Some Strange Dog Owners

My brother Barry and his family paid us a visit towards the end of August. My concern was how Jack would react to Amelia, my niece, who adored him. She had got to know Jack on our visits up north, to sort out my Mum's house and in Wales, when we buried my Mum's ashes. Jack wasn't bothered by her attention then, but now it was different. After his two runs in with the Field Study Centre and groups of screaming children, Jack viewed youngsters with a healthy suspicion, avoiding them at all costs.

It was as I thought. Jack didn't desire any notice from Amelia what so ever, much to her disappointment. Albeit only six years old, she understood when I explained about Jack's bad experiences with children. Most of the day, Jack spent studiously evading Amelia, especially on a walk in the woods. This was one day when Jack stayed close to me for the duration of the outing, refusing to run because he wasn't happy.

However, back in the house, packed into our small dining room eating lunch, Jack lay by Mark, who sat on the floor stroking him, while Tim and Amelia played skittles at the other end of the room; far enough away to present no threat.

Later in the day, as we waved them off calling, "Bye, bye," Jack knew exactly what those words meant and looked hopeful. When their car was out of sight, we entered our garden. "They've gone Jack," I called. Well, you should have seen him go. Full tilt round his racetrack, through the long areas, (cheeky monkey), hairpin bends round trees, celebrating his freedom.

I'm sure Barry, Pat, Tim and Amelia would be quite insulted if they knew, but there's no need. Although Jack's main bugbear was children, adults visiting could equally put him out, if it messed his strict routine up. And if visiting other people, he could be very to the point too. When visiting others, we always took Jack's duvet, so that he could relax instead of standing at their door waiting to go home, no sooner had we got there! Jack would happily sleep, while we talked or watched a film. If he felt it was getting rather late, up he would get to yawn and stretch. "Mer, mer, mer. It's time to go now," he would say. Which we all found quite amusing and none of our hosts minded. They all had a very high regard for Jack.

During late summer, on one of our pre-breakfast, weekend walks, Jack was trotting a few feet ahead of us, the September sun casting a golden glow of peacefulness. "Ow, ow, ow!" Jack yelped out, simultaneously jumping to one side. "Ow, ow, ow, ow!" he yelped, turning his head towards his right side. "Ow, ow, ow!" he kept shouting as he ran off up the track, with Mark on his heels, trying to catch up to find out what the problem could be. "Wait Jack, wait," called Mark. Luckily Jack did wait and Mark saw a large wasp, hanging on just behind Jack's shoulder, continuously stinging. Quickly, Mark flicked the wasp into orbit, as I caught up to examine Jack. Why the wasp stung Jack, is a mystery, as he was walking along minding his own business. With nothing visible and with Jack seeming all right, we finished our walk, going to the walled garden for Mark to feed the birds and open up. Not long after our entry, Jack started to yelp out every now and again and I noticed that the muscles where the wasp had stung him kept going into spasm. "I'd better take him home," I told Mark.

Jack looked very unhappy as we slowly made our way to the house, as walking upset it even more. Once inside, I held an ice pack over the now, very swollen muscles. As the contractions got less, I rubbed Anthisan gently into the skin. When Mark came in, I asked him to go to wherever was open on a Sunday and buy some Waspeze. On his return he reported that no one had any, so he got Bite-ease instead. Hoping it would work, I sprayed Jack's stings straight away. By now his fur in that area looked a complete mess; as long as he was comfortable, that was all that mattered.

After an hour or so, Jack could lie down without leaping up again in sudden pain. By the time two hours had elapsed, the spasms had died away. Gradually, Jack's audacity returned.

The following weekend, the same thing happened again; same time, along the same track and the stings being very close to the original site. I treated Jack as before and he soon recovered, although his confidence in that particular track was in shreds. We avoided that way a few times, as Jack did not want to go there, until one morning when I told them to wait while I went to find if there was a wasp nest. Walking back and to, I finally discovered a tunnel with occasional wasps flying back and forth. Knowing they would be dying off soon anyway, I stuck a big stick up the hole and covered it with leaves.

The next time we ventured that way, I told Jack to wait while I checked the nest, which he did. Everything seemed quiet but to be on the safe side, I told Jack to run with me until we were past the danger zone. Bravely he accompanied me and was pleased to have achieved such a feat. Of course, I hugged him and told him how good he was, which always helps. Eventually, we didn't need to run along that stretch, reverting to our normal pace, any thought of danger banished from our minds, dog scents Jack's main focus.

Some time after these incidents, on an afternoon walk, the three of us were walking down Green Ride, when ahead we could see a couple with a toddler and a greyhound. "Let's walk a bit faster to try and get there before Jack notices," I ventured. Too late. No sooner were the words out of my mouth then Jack took off like a shot, disappearing round the corner which they had just turned. I rushed to catch up, just in time to see Jack barge through, knocking their baby over. As I apologised, the young lady laughed, "It's all right, he's always doing that," she said indicating to her dog.

He was a lovely brindle, similar size to Jack and although of racing stock, had belonged to the man from a puppy. Being castrated, the other greyhound was of no interest to Jack, who trotted along trying to ignore him. The brindle dog however, was delighted to meet Jack and gambolled round him at a respectful distance. The couple said he was normally very quiet and well behaved. It seemed Jack must have awoken something in him, as he went in every puddle, no matter how muddy and ran madly about.

Mind you, Jack very often had this effect on many dogs. I don't know what it was about him. It wasn't as if he wanted them to play. He didn't. He just got on with his own business, the other dog fawning round him. Not that he minded either; secretly, I think the adoration pleased him. If it got a bit out of hand, Jack would stop walking and stand stock still, looking into the distance. The other dog usually then kept a polite distance between them.

As we were on the same path, we walked together. The brindle dog galloped happily ahead and bumped into Daisy and Jaffa, as they rounded a bend. "Have you got another one?" Daisy called out. "No, he belongs to these people," I called back. Jaffa didn't quite know what to think of this dog that bounded round at a worrying speed. Jack had never done that – not with Jaffa anyway.

Jack, in total control, coolly sat down by the side of the path, his back to a tree. Jaffa, after watching the speed of the brindle dog, with a hidden concern, decided it may be safest with Jack and promptly sat down right next to him, for maximum protection. How I wish I'd had a camcorder. His ploy worked though, Jaffa remaining by Jack's side until we parted company.

Another dog, which Jack and I occasionally met, was a small collie lurcher bitch, who was snowy white with black ears, which when not folded down, pricked up in a floppy sort of way, a black patch over her left eye and a wispy broken coat. She was exquisitely beautiful, with a deep chest and tucked up waist. She adored Jack and he was rather taken by her, too.

Chatting to her owner one day, we stood on a woodland track wide enough for a vehicle, while she tried to get Jack to run. He was reluctant, not wishing to get any more injuries but when she tore past him, towards us, I could see Jack decide to show her he could run as well. Revving his engines and accelerating after her, his turbo kicked in and he hurtled past her at nigh on forty miles per hour. She was so shocked, she veered off slamming her brakes on, staring after Jack, in awe. Her owner and I virtually fluttered in the vortex of his wake. Wow! I was rendered speechless. My heart swelled fit to burst – nothing could compare to that feeling. And he was all mine.

It was around this time that Jack and I met Joe and Daisy, two retired greyhounds. Daisy was a small brindle, fine yet well muscled. Joe was big, black with some white, strong and handsome, and both wore muzzles. The first time we met them off the lead, they tore up to Jack growling. Jack jumped off the path giving a small squeak as he did so. "Stand still," I commanded Jack. Their lady owner apologised. "It's all right, he's just getting a taste of his own medicine," I laughed.

Joe and Daisy strutted and posed a little then, as Jack wasn't going to run, walked away. Jack followed, interested yet respectful because he assumed they were both bitches, due to Joe being neutered. Even though Joe had been castrated, you wouldn't have thought so from his behaviour – tail high, eyes wild, cocking his leg high and kicking the ground furiously whilst growling. He made me laugh – he was just like Jack in that respect. Meeting Joe and Daisy brought it home to me how much Jack had calmed down. He seemed so meek and quiet compared to them; he no longer rushed excitedly up to other dogs – meeting other dogs was normal to him. I knew Joe and Daisy would go the same way, in time.

Like with Joe and Daisy's owner, we knew all the locals and their dogs, forming a relationship with them, whether Jack got on with their dog or not. There would be an understanding whereby, when they didn't get on, for instance if Jack was too pushy or certain dogs didn't like big dogs and would go for them, we would wave to each other, call a greeting and go different ways, or both hold onto our dogs if having to pass each other.

Some dog owners, who were on holiday and visiting the estate, exhibited quite strange behaviour, not seeming to understand dogs at all. The usual thing was the silly comments such as, "He'll think my dog's a rabbit," or "He thinks my dog is his lunch," referring to Jack, who was plainly ignoring their small dog or displaying a keen male interest in their unneutered bitch – ears pricked but slightly backward-turned, tail high and waving rapidly at the tip, very bright-eyed and looking his best.

All this was completely lost on them. If he had lowered his head, pricked his ears forward with an intense stare, stood very still, trembling slightly, with his tail at half mast and certainly not waving, then I think they would have been correct.

Some of these people would scoop their little dog up, refusing to put it down, even when I explained that Jack was fine. One girl picked her miniature Dachshund up and held it at head height, although she surprised me by putting it on the ground when I told her that Jack was all right. Jack said a brief hello to the little dog, then trotted off.

One lady screamed and shouted to, 'keep your dog away from mine. Greyhounds kill other dogs'. I talked to her to clarify why people thought that. Her spaniel had no problem with Jack yet she remained convinced that at any minute, Jack could go in for the kill.

Then there were people who chose to retreat through the nearest gate, to avoid their dog coming into contact with Jack. This didn't put him off. Following them, he would touch noses with their dog through the bars of the gate, wave his tail, then walk off. Whether the people thought, "That was all right then," or "Phew, that was a close shave," I'll never know!

Similarly, a group with a Shitzu were approaching through the Deer Park, towards the gate that we were passing. They picked up their dog and instead of exiting they congregated like sheep. "He's all right," I called but they politely refused to come out until Jack and I were well out of the way.

Now and again, we came across people whose dog had been attacked once, previously and their confidence had been shattered – not the dogs', the owners'. The poor dog would be grabbed in a panic, clipped onto the lead then held as close as possible to the owner, hung by the neck, the life being choked out of the unfortunate creature. With its front feet off the ground, the hapless dog would desperately try to look behind it, instinctively knowing that most attacks come from behind, at the same time being scared out of its wits by its owners apparent alarm, yet being completely powerless to do anything to protect itself if necessary.

Jack and I met a couple who demonstrated this sort of behaviour. They had three West Highland white terriers, the husband ahead with one, the woman a few yards behind with two, all on extending leads. Jack, with his ears nearly crossing, quickened his pace. As he neared the dogs he had second thoughts, as the two with the woman barked furiously at him, while the woman shouted. Keeping his gait, he trotted through the middle of them and went to investigate smells some yards away. As the man was busy strangling his dog, I tried to tell him why he shouldn't hang his dog, thus worrying it but to let it meet other dogs. He walked off, as his wife joined in with, "Dogs should be on the lead all the time in here," which wasn't true at all. "Maybe you should let your dogs off," I told her. "I was just trying to tell you about dog behaviour," I called after her. "I know all about dog behaviour," she retorted, as she disappeared down the woodland trail. "I'm quite sure you do," I thought to myself, tongue in cheek.

Because Jack wasn't one for attacking dogs, their dog that was being strangled was in no danger. Unlike a dog in the very same situation. A very credible person related the following story to me. A man, who had a young greyhound, was walking it on the lead. When approached by a Jack Russell, the man held the greyhound on a short lead, tightly, by his legs. In this defenceless position, the greyhound was attacked by the Jack Russell, which fastened itself onto the long tail, mangling it so badly that it had to be amputated. I was quite glad to hear that the vets bill was so huge, the man was unable to pay and had to sign the dog over to the vet to be re-homed. The greyhound became terrified of being on the lead, when meeting other dogs, as the poor thing believed he would be attacked again, with no room for self-defence.

Whilst dog owners who hold their dogs very close, at the approach of another dog, believe they are protecting them, they are in fact making them vulnerable to attack, especially if the approaching dog is a bit of a bully and not very confident; when this type of dog sees another one in a position of vulnerability, it will take full advantage of the opportunity. It is far better to let your dog face them.

After Jack and I met the people with the three West Highland whites, we carried on towards home. Not having progressed too far before we noticed some strange behaviour ahead of us. Two figures with two medium sized dogs on the lead, walking up the path towards us, promptly stepped into the trees, disappearing from view. "They'll be hiding from us Jack," I told him. Having also observed them, as I had, he was just as curious as to what they were doing. He had to investigate. Once we drew level, I could see a woman, a girl and the two dogs standing well back, waiting for us to vacate the wood before they dared venture out. Jack made his way towards them through the long grass. When the dogs barked in a frenzy, he turned round, making his way back to me. The lady said something about her dogs not being too friendly, which was quite plain to see. I suspected that it was not because they were vicious but because they had learnt to view other dogs as a threat by being kept on the lead and not being allowed to socialise.

We met many dogs with the same behavioural problem, which saddened me, as they could, with a little time and patience, become normal, carefree dogs, happy to meet their own kind.

A few yards further, in the meadow, with Jack on the lead, I was talking to Mark whom I had bumped into, telling about these dog-walkers with strange attitudes, when two ladies drew near, accompanied by three Dachshunds on leads. Seeing Jack, they gave us a wide berth. Not that Jack showed any interest in their dogs. Passing us, they muttered apologies and excuses for their dogs, none of which seemed too bothered by Jacks presence. "I've met them all today," I expostulated to Mark, "I'm going home before I meet any more!"

On a different occasion, Mark, Jack and I were setting out on a walk one Sunday, while a musical afternoon concert was being held by the restaurant. As we threaded our way through the onlookers, seated in their picnic chairs on the grass, a dog whose extending lead was loosely tied round a chair leg, leapt up barking and charged straight for Jack. All of us stopping momentarily as the snarling dog reached us. Jack kept his cool, as well as Mark and myself. Instead of attacking, the dog looked extremely surprised at being allowed to get close to Jack, went very quiet and did not know quite what to do. We all walked off with a faint look of disdain on our faces. I suspect that particular dog was one of those which was kept on the lead because it 'barked at others' and 'wasn't friendly'.

There were times when large dogs, such as Labradors, would rush up to

Jack then run off. If they hadn't been neutered, Jack would growl and chase them, to get in front and stop their flight. I would go and restrain Jack whilst the owners beat a hasty retreat. I can thoroughly understand people worrying when another dog growls at theirs. What many people don't realise is that dogs have a variety of growls and most of those do not mean an imminent attack. Greyhounds that have raced quite often use growls in excitement and will talk to their owners in a growly voice; indeed, I have met other dogs that do this too. Having Jack in my life, made me listen to the growls that he and other dogs emitted and to note their behaviour. Jack sometimes growled to himself while in full flight, round the garden, especially on a tight bend.

Most dogs play by the rules but a few don't. Jack was caught out a few times by those who came to greet him, wagging their tail, only to launch an attack once within range. This is sly, learnt behaviour and the main culprits were Labradors and border collies. Luckily Jack was pretty nimble, being able to run out of harms way. These few sly dogs seemed to be visitors to the estate, which we didn't meet again. This behaviour from a few did in no way put Jack off his many Lab and collie friends that he met in the wood.

What amused me were some dog owners' reactions to their dog sniffing Jack's bottom, which is perfectly natural dog behaviour. "Don't do that Sophie, it's dirty!" or "Don't be rude Susie!" Jack didn't mind in the slightest. In fact he must have smelt pretty good, as many bitches idolised him.

One time, Jack and I met a couple with three small dogs on leads. The lady ran off with two of them, when she saw Jack. Her husband was more laid back, carrying on his normal pace with his little fluffy terrier, wearing a tartan coat. Jack trotted up to sniff delicately and wave his tail with pleasure, while the little dog was equally pleased at the meeting. The woman watched from a safe distance, probably with a thudding heart.

Many were the people who had a strange mind-set towards their rescue dogs. While on holiday in Wales, on one of our beach walks, Jack was approaching a large mongrel, which was on the lead. The man in charge grabbed it to him when he spotted Jack's advance, backing into the sea, as if to somehow erect a barrier between them. The waves were no deterrent to Jack, who soon reached the two. Another strangling case was set in motion, as the man hung his dog as best he could, shoving Jack away with his free hand. By this time Mark had reached the trio and paddled into the sea to remove Jack and allow the man and dog to make their way onto the beach once more. Mark reported the man said the dog was a stray and he didn't know what it would do. He was unlikely to find out by preventing it from meeting other dogs, was he now! The sad thing was, his dog really looked as though it would have liked to meet Jack.

I met many people in our wood who never let their dog off the lead and when I enquired as to why, was duly informed, "It's a rescue." Ah, I see.

So, does that mean they are incapable of learning any new sets of rules and grasping commands? Admittedly, any dog that exhibits considerable fearfulness shouldn't be let off, especially in an unfamiliar place, until if ever, its confidence has been restored. Sadly, the dogs that Jack and I met were in no way fearful but looked eagerly about, longing to meet others and explore. It was their owners who needed confidence in their ability to control their dog.

Thank goodness we didn't come across aggressive owners often. While I was standing chatting to a couple who had the most beautiful standard poodle, Jack was chatting to the poodle. Both dogs trotted around giving the odd growl now and then. As we were standing on the main woodland walk path, people and dogs passed us at intervals. A man and a woman were walking towards us with a flat-coated retriever off the lead. The man took one look at Jack and his friend and put his dog on the lead, telling it in a very stern voice to walk right by his side. The poor dog, showing the whites of its eyes, looked quite worried. The woman walked by the other side of the dog, effectively sandwiching it, so it could not watch its back. Jack left the poodle, strode up towards the retriever, barged the woman completely out of the way, nearly overbalancing her, which was quite rude really, and proceeded to try to bar the dogs way. The man lashed the free end of his dog's lead, in a very threatening gesture, growling at Jack to, "Get out of the way." Not wishing any harm to come to Jack, I hurried to get him, telling the man, "Don't be stupid." He informed me that my dog should be on a lead. I replied that his dog would be better off the lead. The couple I was chatting to agreed, saying that most dogs sort themselves out. One thing's for certain – dogs understand their own language better than humans do.

In the earlier days, Jack was in the wood with Mark and I, ahead as usual, when I spotted a man's head above the bracken and brambles, on the other side of a rise in the ground. Jack also saw him and hurried forward to check out if he had a dog. Speeding up, I went after Jack. I guessed correctly that a dog was involved due to the man standing stock-still. As I rounded the corner of the path, there was Jack posing, posturing and growling round a yellow Labrador male that was on the lead, the poor man frozen with fear. Running up I grabbed for Jack's coat but he neatly slipped out of my way. As I told him off, he trotted off to cock his leg on a tree, with much kicking and scraping of the ground, accompanied by growling, sending debris flying through the air, putting on a good show. Apologising to the man, who remained completely silent, I got hold of Jack. The man, seizing his chance, ran off with his dog, never to be seen again!

Around the same period, Jack and I were on our main walk, when ahead of us was a seat occupied by a woman. By her was an elderly lady in a wheelchair, a black Labrador bitch and a German shepherd. Jack's gaze fell upon the dogs and he trotted determinedly straight towards them.

Recognising the group, I realised I had seen them at a distance on their arrival in the car park; Satan, the Manchester terrier, running up behind them and nipping the German shepherd on the back leg. The woman on the seat noticed Jack and leapt up shrieking continuously, causing her dogs to jump as she frantically put them on their leads. Did she think Jack was Satan, who had grown six fold in the past half hour and come looking for her dogs? Jack visibly faltered in his pace, ears flicking and started to give the woman a wide berth. Then, as the woman's back was turned and all had gone quiet, he decided it was safe enough to check out the German shepherd. This put the woman into a blind panic when she turned and saw Jack. Resuming her shrieking, she ran off with the dogs into the wood, abandoning the old lady in the wheelchair, who, having her back to all this, wasn't really aware of the ensuing mayhem. Jack stood staring in amazement. "Come on Jack, this way," I called and after a moment, he trotted after me with a puzzled look on his face. "There's some funny people about Jack," I commented. You know, I'm sure he agreed.

CHAPTER 11

Gunshots and Fireworks

In the September, we went to a large country fair, as the weather promised to be dry and it had been postponed the previous year due to foot and mouth. Parking was organised on grassland and on climbing down from the Land Rover, I could hear shotguns half a mile away, taking part in clay pigeon shooting. I knew Jack wouldn't be happy.

His excitement and eagerness to get out of the vehicle were soon stripped away by the resounding bangs across the parkland. Within seconds, Jack was shaking like a leaf and wanting desperately to get back into the Land Rover. Mark had to hold Jack's lead due to his furious pulling, in an effort to escape. On a short lead, Jack had to walk at a steady pace by our sides, while we told him it was all right, in happy tones.

Mark and I both had to use the Portaloo, so took turns to hold onto Jack, who had calmed down somewhat. Continuing to praise him, we walked to where the main arena and stalls were, which was over a rise in the land. Once over this rise, we could no longer hear the guns and Jack relaxed, becoming interested in other sights, sounds, smells, meeting other dogs and being much admired.

The guns were still shooting on our return to the Land Rover. Jack was far more composed but still glad to get into the safety of our trusty vehicle, nevertheless.

Since then, whenever we heard shotguns while walking in our woods, Jack wasn't so concerned, sometimes not noticing them at all. Apart from one time, that is.

Shooting broke out about half a mile away across the field, by the village, which was too close for Jack's comfort. Off he cantered through the trees and across the heathland. We called but we knew it was no use; he wasn't going to come back towards the guns. Mark and I hurried through the heathland, wondering just how far Jack would have gone. This was unusual for him, as he normally never ran more than a few yards if something upset him.

When we came out onto Green Ride, there was Jack waiting for us. "Come on, hurry up," he indicated, trotting off urgently. The further we went, the calmer he became, resuming his sniffing, marking and kicking.

Talking of calm, I'm reminded of a particular early morning walk with Jack. We had finished the walk, come through the gate between the wood and the meadow, when Jack found a singularly succulent patch of grass, right by the gate post, on which he proceeded to chew. He liked his grazing, so it looked like I was in for a long wait.

Leaning back against the gate, I admired the clear blue sky and early morning light along with various bird sounds coming to me across the still air. Just as I was beginning to wonder if Jack would leave room for his breakfast, the barn owl appeared, floating over the meadow. How glad I was that I was already quiet and still. Back and to he flew, listening for small rodents. When he started to fly towards us, I hoped that Jack wouldn't decide to walk off. Not much chance of that – he was still busy chewing! On came the owl and to my great surprise, just kept coming straight up the path. A few yards – surely he'll see us and veer off. A few feet. Closer he came, quite low and as he advanced, I was able to observe that he was concentrating his gaze on Jack. Flying right up to us, he looked hard at Jack to make sure he wasn't some giant vole, then flew two feet above my head, turned and flew into the Deer Park, without a sound or disturbance of the air!

What an experience! I'd never been so close to a wild barn owl before and I suspect, nor had Jack. The only difference was, Jack had been completely unaware of his presence. I'm sure if Jack had looked up at the last minute, seeing an owl fixing him with a stare, at close quarters, would have spooked him.

Jack grazed on grass almost daily. Usually this was just as a tonic. Sometimes it was to make him sick. He was sick more often than I would have liked and on some of these days, when I put his breakfast down, he would approach, crying to me, telling me that he didn't feel well. More often than not, if I hand fed him, he would eat his food and seem perfectly fine after a sleep.

On our main walks, Jack was now thoroughly trustworthy or rather, I knew him inside out, so could predict him. There had been three occasions only when Jack had been determined to go a different route to me and no amount of stern 'NO's' had any effect. He would look at me as if to say, "It's all right, I know where I'm going. I'll meet you at the other end." I knew what he was saying but I didn't agree with him being on his own.

"Little swine," I muttered to myself, as I carried on along my track. Hurrying slightly, I made sure I met Jack at the other end. No shouting. In fact, not a word at all. Definitely, no smacking either. On went his lead. Held close to my hip to prevent any sniffing, weeing or any other activity; i.e. no freedom; no choice; I walked him back the way he had just come, briskly and in a way, unceremoniously. Then, onto the track he should have accompanied me on, in the first place. Still on a very short lead of about three inches, we marched along until we came to the end where we met. A little further we went, before I took the lead off, releasing him.

This method worked a treat. It made it very clear to Jack, that if he went off on his own, then he would have to go back over his tracks, therefore completely wasting his time and energy. And believe me, he hated doing that! That's why it only happened three times and only then with many months in between.

Jack usually trotted ahead of me but on certain tracks, he did not do much sniffing, which meant his pace far out-stripped mine. I would call out, "Jack wait." He would stop and turn to look at me momentarily, before hurrying on. He knew what 'wait' meant – he just did not want to – partly because he was impatient and partly because I was still walking towards him. If I had changed direction, he would have come after me. Cursing him under my breath, I would jog after him a short way. I could see that outside and off the lead, Jack saw himself as being in charge, to an extent, whereas in the house, he was more amenable.

When it came to pointing, Jack regarded this with two views. If either Mark or I pointed to a piece of toast crust, which Jack couldn't see on the patterned carpet, he would look at the pointing hand and not where we were indicating. I suspect this is because he associated an outstretched hand with food morsels and so concentrated in case another piece of food was forthcoming.

On my walks with Jack, as he was usually ahead of me, I had to indicate to him my intended route. As he approached a junction, I would call, "Jack, this way," clearly denoting with an outstretched arm, to the right or left. After looking at me for a moment, he would then go in the direction I had indicated. I had never taught him this, it's just something I had done with Jim and I saw no reason why Jack couldn't do it as well. I had always told Jack, "This way," or suggested, "Shall we go this way?" whenever we turned at a junction, so he already related the words with changing direction. I just added the arm signals at a later date.

There was the occasional time when Jack looked as though he was about to walk across my raised borders, from the lawn and jump down near the house. He knew he shouldn't do this but liked to tease me at times. If I was outside, I would tell him, "Don't even think about it. Use the steps." When I looked at the steps and pointed, he still had that cheeky look but he would use the steps. Pointing at the steps as I spoke would help to re-enforce my meaning.

Wishing to learn something about greyhound racing, I bought a copy of Greyhound Monthly. If anyone had asked me how long it took a greyhound to run round a 500-metre track, I'm quite sure I would have been miles from the correct figure. About thirty seconds. That's all it takes – very impressive!

While reading this magazine, I found an article by Anne Finch of Greyhounds in NEED, which greatly interested me, and wishing to know more, I contacted them. After sending my subscription, I received a riveting newsletter containing many stories, some upsetting, some very happy and a tributes page. One particular poem, in tribute to a greyhound that had died, really made me think.

If I Knew

If I knew it would be the last time that I'd see you fall asleep,
I would tuck you in more tightly and pray the Lord, your soul to keep.

If I knew it would be the last time that I see you walk out of the door,
I would give you a hug and kiss and call you back for more.

If I knew it would be the last time I'd hear your voice lifted up in praise,
I would videotape each action and word, so I could play them back day
after day.

If I knew it would be the last time, I could spare an extra minute
To stop and say, "I love you," instead of assuming you would know I do.

If I knew it would be the last time I would be there to share your day,
Well I'm sure you'll have so many more, so I can just let this one slip
away.

For surely there's always tomorrow to make up for an oversight,
And we always get a second chance to make everything just right.

There will always be another day to say, "I love you,"
And certainly there's another chance to say, "Anything I can do?"

But just in case I might be wrong, and today is all I get,
I'd like to say how much I love you and I hope we never forget.

Tomorrow is not promised to anyone, young or old alike,
And today may be the last chance you get to hold your loved one tight.

So if you're waiting for tomorrow, why not do it today?
For if tomorrow never comes, you will surely regret the day,

That you didn't take that extra time for a smile, a hug, or a kiss
And you were too busy to grant someone, what turned out to their one last
wish.

So hold your loved ones close today, and whisper in their ear,
Tell them how much you love them and that you'll always hold them
dear.

Take time to say, "I'm sorry," "Please forgive me," "Thank you," or "It's okay."
And if tomorrow never comes, you will have no regrets about today. [1]

It suddenly hit me that although I adored Jack so much, I had never told him. I felt shocked. Right away I brought a new routine into my life by telling Jack how much I loved him, so many times a day. "I do love you Jack," I would say, as he lay in his bed gazing at me. "You're my special boy," I would continue, going over to sit by him, to put my arms around him, whispering my words and kissing his head. I knew he understood.

Our holiday in Wales came rather late, due to the house being booked up. It was mid October that found me packing our food boxes in our spare bedroom. Jack had one box all to himself, for his food, nail clippers, tick removers, towels, coats, poo bags etc. Three boxes in all sat on the floor, full of food. Jack liked to inspect them politely, never interfering or attempting to take anything edible, even his own food, which was easily accessible.

The day we travelled was very cold and frosty. Unfortunately, this wasn't to last. Rain fell most days. This was not the most relaxing of holidays, due to my having to visit the records office in Caernarfon and the National Library of Wales in Aberystwyth. Mark waited with Jack, in the Land Rover, taking him walks between showers.

We made up for all this sitting about by countless beach walks, where Jack ran and ran to his hearts content. Weather wise, the best day was Thursday when Carol and Eric visited. That only left Friday to carry out Mark's wish to climb Snowdon, and the forecast was awful!

Strong winds, rain and sleet lashed the mountain as we approached. My heart really wasn't in it. Before my back was bad, I'd climbed many times and today, I recommended the Pyg Track, as in my memory, it wasn't too demanding. Well, so much for the memory of someone who wasn't as able as they used to be. Although some stone steps marked the route, mostly the path was made up of huge boulders at odd angles, making stepping up rather high, and coupled with gale force winds, staying upright was extremely difficult.

Jack was on the lead. Even so, this did not prevent him nearly blowing over or from threatening to blow clear away. Nor did it stop his feet slipping and sliding, as he desperately tried to grip using his nails, which could get no purchase on the wet rock. I felt terrible, as I tried to help him. What had I got him into? Banging his knee as he slipped; scratching his inner thigh – he was still game and eager to explore further.

Looking back down, I realised it would be worse to try and climb down again. Once over the ridge it would be much easier, as far as I could remember. When one is fit, a lot of things seem easy! My relief at eventually reaching the ridge was short-lived. On the other side, two tall stiles barred the path. "They weren't here last time I came up," I remarked to Mark, "You're going to have to carry Jack over." "He won't like that," he replied. "I know but there's no other way," I said, feeling a bit fed up. Mark removed his rucksack, leaving it on the track. It's lucky there were two stiles, as it made out job easier – Mark climbed one with Jack in his arms, so was unable to see where to place his feet. I walked up the other, guiding his boots onto each step and making sure he didn't fall. Safely on the other side, rucksack re-instated, we resumed our trek.

For short intervals, the track was effortless. Unfortunately, the majority of the time, it was no better than our original climb. The wind never let up and periodically, we endured hail blasting into our faces. Jack was wearing his winter coat with the hood up, yet I wished he was better protected.

The further we went, the more arduous it seemed. My back was so tired, it was ready to snap in two. It was dawning on Jack that there may be no end to this walk and his interest was ebbing away. Stopping to blow my nose, I looked up. The summit appeared to be still so distant. I noticed Jack surveying the walkers ahead, as they snaked along the side of the mountain, then scanning up to the summit; the look on his face said it all – good grief, we're not going all the way up there, are we? Oh Jack, I know just how you feel – utterly defeated!

The hail stopped; the cloud lifted and a ray of sunshine illuminated the surrounding peaks, as we struggled a little further. "Take a picture of Jack and I, while the sun's out," I said, happy to have a rest. On attempting to set the lens reading, Mark discovered that the light meter had broken, so guesswork came into play. While he took a number of shots at varying apertures, it was clear that Jack was completely fed up, turning from nose pointing up the track, to leaning on my leg and eventually, nose pointing down the track. He'd had enough and so had I. "I can't go any further and nor can Jack. Do you mind if we go down the track we passed a bit ago, down to the lakes?" I beseeched Mark. "No, that's all right," he said, "We'll go down."

The 'track' we had seen, was very vague to say the least. I had experienced it years before and did not relish the idea. Cairns littered the scree slope in a jumble, where previous walkers had passed, yet there was no path to speak of – just downward, as carefully as possible!

Jack had to be helped frequently and became more fractious the further we descended, refusing to budge at times. Two thirds of the way down, we came across a work party constructing steps, which would ultimately join the Miner's Track below, to the Pyg Track above. We were extremely grateful to be allowed the use of these lower steps, to gain the shores of the lake – the end to scrambling and slipping on loose rocks.

Mark and I sat on a large piece of slate, while Jack curled up very small, on the only patch of grass nearby, which was only just big enough. Kendal Mint Cake, a hot drink and nutty bars covered in glucose, tasted wonderful. Jack was most unimpressed with the smell of the mint cake, refusing to accept any but had a drink of water.

Our remaining descent was more gentle, winding past Llyn Lydaw, the surface under our feet, almost like stone sets. Though this track was considerably easier, Jack and I found it hard to appreciate, along with the beautiful scenery – we were running on empty. Finally, we stumbled into the car park at Pen-y-Pass, ready to sink down. How Jack mustered the strength to jump into the Land Rover, escapes me. Flinging himself down in exhaustion, he closed his eyes. Mark and I both needed to empty our bladders and made our way to the toilets. I looked back to see Jack's anguished face staring out of the rear window. He didn't have long to wait. Still, it seemed long enough to my back before I could collapse into my seat. "Never again," I thought, "Never again."

While I knew my back would take many months to revert to normal levels of pain, I fervently hoped that Jack had not been affected, yet feared he somehow would be. Sitting for many hours for our journey back east, was very welcome to myself and Jack; both resembling zombies.

Back to normality, Jack seemed fine until the 2nd November. Mark took him out for their usual nightly perambulations. Unfortunately, as they entered the main car park, a car entered the far end, stopping suddenly. Someone got out then quickly got back in, the car driving off just as an air-bomb exploded, the sound reverberating far into the night. I heard it as I was putting some rubbish into the bin, outside the back door. My heart sank. Minutes later, Jack dragged Mark to the back door, and on my opening it, rushed frantically in, staring wildly.

I didn't fuss but carried on as normal, apart from the fact that I put the radio on. I went through the usual routines with Jack; biscuits, teeth cleaning – it's not easy to listen intently while your teeth are being scrubbed – ointment and a massage. With confidence returning, we went to bed, Jack quite glad that he now slept upstairs.

As the weather was colder, another sheepskin had been purchased for Jack for his upstairs bed. A lovely taupe, it was placed ceremoniously in the bed with Jack being invited to climb in and lie down. He gazed with adoration and appreciation up into Mark's face, as if to say, "Thank you Daddy. A sheepskin upstairs as well, to keep me warm and comfy. It's lovely, thank you."

During that night Jack got us up to do a poo in the garden, due to him not having done anything at all before the fireworks had frightened him, during the evening. The following evening, all was quiet and Jack successfully completed his walk. However, the 4th November was a repeat of the 2nd, with air-bombs being let off just as Jack had begun his walk. The next three nights, fireworks were heard and no matter how distant, Jack did not want to go out.

Jack clearly was able to tell the difference between gunshots and fireworks and in his eyes, fireworks were far worse. For many weeks, Jack did not look forward to his evening walk, staying in his big bed. He would listen intently at the open back door, for any hint of a bang. Even though none were heard, his walk would be carried out fleetingly, filled with trepidation, only feeling secure, once back in the house. Jack never hid or cringed, when he heard fireworks from indoors, although he did look concerned. The longer the period with no explosions, Jack's eagerness returned for his nightly explorations with Mark, once more being absorbed by dog and rabbit scents.

Two weeks since our return from Wales, we were due to go up north for a week. I had great difficulty finding affordable accommodation where a dog was accepted. A barn conversion, consisting of two cottages by the owner's house, had a 'dog' sign, so I provisionally booked it, while Mark sorted out time off work.

Meanwhile, my cousin Carol, had visited the said cottages to have a look and informed me that the 'lady' had told her, 'the dog will have to sleep in the barn'. Incensed, I rang the woman and told her, "My dog doesn't sleep in a barn." I wouldn't heap such indignity on Jack, being so fastidious and clean. He would have been wounded deeply, had we abandoned him in a flea-ridden barn, with straw for a bed, in place of his wool blankets and sheepskins. He was no tramp and I would not treat him like one.

After I had listed his qualities, the woman said, "Well, all right then," and we arranged the date. Some days later, when no directions arrived, I telephoned. "Oh, we don't normally send anything out," came the surprising reply, to my enquiry. Eventually, a photocopy of a road atlas page arrived, which was just enough for us to be able to search a given area for the property. I must admit, I did have some misgivings.

Luckily, we had bought an old ordnance survey map of the area and used this, on our arrival, as we drove up this road and down that one, round and about, asking a lady down a lane if she knew of the place. She directed us to our cottage, where no one was there to greet us. As the correspondence had not named which cottage we were in, we had to discern this ourselves, wandering round the back of the building to discover ours; the one without the first floor.

Being open, Mark unloaded while I searched high and low for a heating control. I was frozen and so were the radiators. Everything in, darkness fell and I was desperately cold. Two trips to the house and calling out round the stables, showed no one was about, apart from a large German shepherd in the barn.

I decided to look in the other cottage. The central heating boiler and controls were just inside the door, so I turned up the heat. Soon, warmth flooded our radiators and we turned from blue to pink. "Let's have some pasta," I said to Mark, who eagerly agreed. Searching the kitchen cupboards, no pans were really big enough. The largest was rusty inside. Disgusting! There was no way I was going to use that.

Once again, I went round to the house, where I was lucky enough to catch the woman and her family, who had just come home from a days shopping. We introduced ourselves, shaking hands then I told her about the pans and heating. She seemed quite insulted that I had any complaint about the pans but duly lent me a couple of large ones from the other cottage, which were in suitable condition. With regards to the heating, she was quite angry, turning the boiler down again, to my horror. "What if it goes off again?" I asked. "Come and tell me. It shouldn't do. You shouldn't have turned it up full, it could have blown up," she rather petulantly told me. Well, surely that boiler is a health hazard, not complying with health and safety, if it's likely to blow up!

Then came the sledgehammer. "Oh, would you keep your dog in the kitchen," she said bluntly, referring to a tiny room, with a tiled floor, full of our food boxes, boots and no room to swing a cat. "No. He's not sleeping in the kitchen," I replied. "It's what we agreed," she lied, (and a policeman's wife too!) "It is NOT," I said emphatically. "Yes it is," she countered. "No, it certainly is NOT," I replied, in a very determined fashion. "Well, I'm not falling out with you," she said and walked off to her house. Returning to Mark and Jack, I related my story. Mark was incredulous.

To our relief, the heating stayed on, though the timing was not in our control. Oh, and the cooker door fell to pieces when I opened it. Still, beggars can't be choosers. Above our heads, hanging on the wall from chains, was an old rusty scythe, which was reminiscent of the grim reaper and I was worried that it may slip off one of its chains and decapitate me during the night!

Our stay there was not a happy one. There was nowhere to walk Jack, apart from around the local roads, where we ran the gauntlet of mad drivers. Jack could have been let off in the paddock at the back of the holiday lets but this was very muddy and Jack would have found it even more boring than the roads. I spent most of the week washing Jack's feet and legs anyway and wiping the kitchen floor. The cottage was far cleaner when we left it, than it was when we arrived. All of us were never more pleased to leave a place, rejoicing to be going back home.

The last week in November and the first week in December, Jack woke us virtually every night, for various reasons. To be covered with his blanket because it had fallen off when he got up to shake, before lying down again; to go downstairs for a drink of water; to go downstairs and eat some of his biscuits; for a look round the garden, sometimes doing a poo; to check on a rabbit he'd caught the same day and make sure no one had dug it up and stolen it. One evening, after catching a rabbit and bringing it home, Jack left it on the lawn, which was unusual. During the night, he insisted on going downstairs. It was assumed he was desperate for the toilet yet when Mark came back to bed, he informed me that Jack had buried his rabbit. He must have remembered during the night and started worrying that it wasn't hidden.

One or two of these nights, Jack decided to sleep downstairs, which felt quite strange to us, now that we were used to him being upstairs. Later, he would wake me with his plaintive whine, asking to come up, halfway through the night.

Also at this time, Jack had begun to have difficulty bending his head down to sniff, eat or drink, or to lift his head from lying down, squeaking out loudly. I worried that this was due to the trauma his muscles and joints had gone through on Snowdon. Every day I gave Jack a massage, after walks. When I sat on a chair to remove my Wellingtons, he would stand between my knees, quite often before I was ready, to receive his rubdown. First his shoulders, then neck and all along either side of his spine, finishing with his thighs.

This treatment did help, although periodically Jack would have a few days and nights where he would squeak out in pain. We bought a feeding stand to put his food bowl in, to make things more comfortable when eating. There were times when I asked Jack to sit, that he dipped his bottom slightly floorwards, then back up again, at the same time, talking to me. Was he trying to tell me it hurt him to sit down or was he just being awkward? He still sat in the garden of his own accord, so I wasn't sure. I suspected it was painful to sit at times, therefore I didn't make him do so, if he didn't want to.

Jack's water bowl remained on the floor. He normally drank after a walk or after food, when I was always with him. As soon as he began to have these difficulties, I used to say, "Wait a minute. Let me help you," and proceeded to pick his water bowl up, holding it, enabling him to drink. He got so used to this, that he would stand by his bowl and turn to look at me, as if to say, "Will you help me?" If I was not in the kitchen and heard a little squeak, I would call out for him to wait, while I rushed to his aid.

Over the Christmas period, Mark and I decorated the hall, stairs and landing, painstakingly stripping the inside of the front door of paint. Having removed all bolts and catches, the only security was a long piece of wood, propped under the old rim lock and butted up to the foot of the stairs. Jack found this a bit of an inconvenience, as he distrustfully assumed it may fall on him. Each time he accompanied me up and down the stairs, I had to lift the wood out of his way.

The day the walls had been painted a primrose yellow, Jack backed up into a corner while I lifted the wood for his safe passage. Later, I noticed some marks on the stripped door. On closer inspection, these revealed themselves as paint, brushed on by Jack's tail. Ah, I'd better look at his tail.

Sure enough, yellow paint decorated his black fur. He hated his tail to be held. Nevertheless, I removed the paint using paraffin. Afterwards, wiping with soapy water to leave his tail more acceptable to him.

Between the decorating, we did manage a meal at Richard's and a meal at Leigh's. Jack was invited to both 'do's', lying quietly on his duvet asleep, apart from when food was being moved about. Richard came with us to Leigh's, where Wendy, Leigh's partner, cooked a lovely meal, Leigh sneaked tit-bits to Jack, which he shouldn't have, and later we all enjoyed watching 'Lord of the Rings'.

As soon as the film had finished, then Jack informed us it was time to go home. And who were we to argue?

CHAPTER 12

Pain and Love

Regardless of my massaging, Jack still seemed troubled with soreness during January, crying out while lowering his head when standing or when lifting it from lying down. Limping and stiffness accompanied the crying out, after rest.

During mid January, Jack had pulled up short, limping after a small run. I wasn't sure if he'd strained muscles when he stopped quickly, or if pain had put paid to his run. Two days later, a large bruise was discovered at the top of Jack's front left leg, just on his chest. Not seeing him hit anything, I was mystified as to how it had happened. We shortened our walks and Jack soon returned to a normal gait. Each time he did this, I presumed he was back to his previous fitness.

Jack no longer ran madly, nor had his early morning burn-up. Plodding behind me, I assumed he had calmed down. Still, something niggled inside me.

However, Jack was still catching rabbits. Near the end of January, Mark had taken Jack for his last walk of the day and being that particular time of the year, the darkness was thick and black. As there was no livestock in the church field, Jack was let off his lead to travel at his own speed. Up to the church, a look round the trees outside the churchyard, then walk back. Mark was half way along the track heading home, when Jack ran past him, coat hanging off, carrying a big rabbit in his mouth. Completely unaware of any activity or drama having taken place, Mark was surprised to say the least. Managing to get Jack to come to him, Mark straightened the coat, re-fastening the strap. The coat was covered in mud. Jack was allowed to bring his rabbit home, to bury.

After putting the coat straight into the washing machine, I checked Jack all over. Although I found no injuries, I was worried. Did he fall or slide, while putting so much effort into his catch, or did he snag his coat on something? It was a big adult rabbit. Adults are usually very experienced in evading capture, so Jack's effort must have been considerable.

That night, Jack woke me three times, yelping out in pain. Getting out of bed, I would rub his neck gently and cover him up with his blanket. Over the next four days it was the same story; lots of squeaks and yelps. I stepped up my massage, with Jack requesting more when he wanted it. It must have afforded him some relief, otherwise he wouldn't have asked for more. Jack wasn't just mithering to be stroked – he wasn't that sort of dog.

He very rarely stood by either Mark's or my chair, to be petted.

Things did ease up over the next few weeks, but never entirely went away. On one occasion, Jack was having difficulty with his rear legs, while trying to lie down. Although suspecting a back problem, I left it a little longer, in case it cleared up. If a further bad session occurred, I would seek professional help.

All this time, Jack's pyoderma had begun to worsen, bleeding on a daily basis, so I had this on my mind. The vet arranged for Jack to see a dermatologist, who took various samples and discussed several options in treatment. A few days later, our vet phoned with the specialists report – anti-bacterial cream and very strong anti-biotics for three weeks. Having made it clear to the consultant, that I preferred natural methods, I told my vet that I would try one of the discussed options, plus manuka honey, first. He agreed that I could do this and I set to work immediately.

The consultant had discussed a natural source vitamin E and this is what I used; one capsule daily in Jack's food, in conjunction with Manukacare 18+, a sterilised honey used in some hospitals, applied three times a day, directly to the inside of the prepuce.

Within three weeks, the improvement was remarkable and over the following weeks, the skin healed fully, looking better than I had ever seen it. This treatment was for life – as long as the skin stayed healthy, I didn't mind. It was one thing less to worry about.

John and Jenny, the elderly couple we knew, had lost Gemma, their little foxy dog, who had adored Jack. After paying them a visit to commiserate with them over losing Gemma, we were all congregating in their hallway, before our departure. Happening to glance into their convex mirror, which acted like a fish-eye lens, I could see the entire group squashed together in the reflected image. Seeing Jack's image, I leaned closer to the mirror, "Hello Jack," I said, waving at him. He did a double take, then going towards the mirror, reared up on his hind legs, being careful not to put his feet onto either the shelf beneath, which held small china ornaments, or the radiator, he peered into the mirror. I wonder what went through his mind when he saw all of us standing at a distance, through a round 'window'. I peered in beside him, so that he could see my image alongside his. He seemed satisfied then, that all was as it should be. I must say though, that his notice of our far away, concentrated image, was quite acute and this astounded me somewhat.

The spring brought all the birdwatchers to the wood, especially into the Deer Park. Jack and I would come across ones or twos or sometimes groups, standing loosely, staring in different directions. Jack quite often made a point of strolling through the middle of the party, selecting a suitable marking point a little farther on, cocking his leg, to follow up with scuffing and kicking, whilst giving a sidelong look at them, before strolling after me. He did make me smile.

Being March, we also experienced fog on some of our pre-breakfast walks. By now, we did not need our big torch; the sun was already above the horizon. The fog was quite thick in places, casting an eerie stillness to the dripping wood. Just as we were about to head home, on one of these days, Jack suddenly locked onto a scent, which sent him round in circles, figures of eight, diving back and to across the ride, nose to the ground. Rearing up on his hind legs, Jack looked over the brambles and dead bracken. Why did he not look into the Deer Park? And why did he only look over the undergrowth? He had not stood upright since we first had him and then he was on the lead. What was he expecting to see?

While I was busy deliberating, Jack shot off into the mist, along the track towards the back of the farm. Not expecting him to have gone far, I called him. Nothing but silence and drips. Tutting to myself, I jogged the route Jack had taken, calling as I ran. On reaching a junction, I didn't know which way he had gone, so I stopped to wait, still calling, "Jack, Jack."

Not being able to see very far was not helping matters. Knowing it was better to stay put, I called and called until, in a mad flurry, Jack nearly ran past. Slamming his brakes on, he dashed to me, pleased yet apologetic. "Good boy, good boy," I praised, as I gave him a hug. Although I asked him what he had gone after, he wasn't able to tell me. I always wondered if it was a fox, yet whenever he saw one, he thought it was a dog. Or, was it Bracken, and had Jack stood up high to look over the undergrowth, to see if he could see Bracken on the path, round the corner?

Bracken was a golden retriever male, who still retained his manhood and Jack loved to tease him. Bracken didn't stand for too much nonsense, although he accepted that Jack was in charge, due to his ability to jump about athletically in front of the other dog.

Jack ran off again on another foggy morning and when I finally caught up with him, he was doing a growly dance round Bracken and his owner, Les. I enquired of Les if they had been in the wood the other morning, when Jack had disappeared into the fog. They had not, so my mystery remained.

Taxa, the big Labrador male, whom Jack also liked to tease, was only met with on occasion now, due to our main walk being changed to the morning. It was on the weekend walks, which were still taken in the afternoon, that we met Bob and Taxa.

I knew that Jack was not hostile towards Taxa, otherwise he would have attacked in the early days. It was clear to me that he was playing silly beggars and I presumed that given time, Jack would grow tired with his game and calm down. There had been a period when Bob and I would go different routes, to keep Jack away from Taxa. When we did meet along a track, I would tell Jack to wait, which he did, then I held his collar, while Bob held Taxa. When we stood chatting, Jack was unable to wind Taxa up and both dogs looked bored and fed up.

By the spring of 2003, Jack could meet Taxa without bothering him, both dogs standing around, while Bob talked to Mark and I. Although Jack still teased Bracken, I guessed it was because he hadn't known him as long as he'd known Taxa.

On our early morning weekend walks, we had been bumping into George, a widower of pensionable age, who owned a delightful Border terrier bitch, called Jenny. Small and very lively, Jenny was kept on an extending lead, otherwise she would have disappeared in the blink of an eye and George could not have run after her.

Jenny wagged her tail, standing on her back legs at the end of her lead, when she saw us – she had to say hello. Jack received the same treatment, only more so. Jenny loved to see Jack. I had assumed she was the same with other dogs, but George informed me that this was not the case. Jenny was indifferent towards most other dogs, especially big ones, putting her tail down and looking into the distance, keeping well out of the way.

As Jenny had been spayed and she tried to dance round Jack, he only said hello with a little wag of his tail, before skipping out of her way. He only gave a brief greeting to spayed bitches and avoided boisterous behaviour. I always worried that the extending lead would get caught round Jack's legs and one day it did.

Jack had stayed on the path to say hello to George. Jenny ran underneath Jack and round his legs. Jack jumped round as he felt the string-like lead on his legs. "Ow, ow, ow," he yelped. George dropped the lead, which enabled Jack to jump away. George apologised profusely, as I handed the lead back and went to look at Jack, putting my arms around him. His legs looked fine – I could not see any damage and took it for granted that Jack was just shouting out in case he got hurt.

Later that day, when Jack was lounging on his back, with his legs in the air, I was horrified to see extensive bruising in his groin area and all down his inner thighs. Poor Jack. It really must have hurt at the time. Those extending leads can do a lot of damage. I know of a man who lost half a finger when his dog took off, with the lead wrapped round his finger.

I never told George, as he would have been mortified that he had hurt Jack in any way. I just made sure that Jack kept out of the way, which he did of his own accord, refusing to say hello to George. If people who use extending leads, reeled their dogs in when they met other dogs, these sort of accidents would not happen.

Rowan's birthday was in March and Mary always held Rowan's Coffee Morning, to raise money for a local animal rescue, as close to his birthday as possible. Jack always attended his friend's birthday party, along with Mark and I. This year Rowan was four.

Either we were late or everyone else was early. When we made our entrance, the room was full of people sitting at tables. "Hello," we said. "Hello Jack," came many voices. All eyes had turned to Jack. People who had never seen him before, stared in admiration, wanting to meet this magnetic animal. Jack seemed as though he felt quite honoured and went sweetly round, greeting friends and strangers graciously. I followed, holding the other end of his lead and was quite glad to eventually sit down, to rest my back.

Someone gave Rowan a squeaky toy, which he proceeded to assault our ears with the whole time. Every now and again, he would march past Jack, showing off his prize. Jack didn't particularly like squeaky toys. He did not equate the not-so-animal-like squeak with the definitely not-very-animal-like object. He just could not make sense of them. Firstly, they were inanimate and secondly, the sound wasn't one he recognised, even though he had heard them in the pet shop.

I took Jack to see what Rowan was up to, as he seemed to think that Rowan was surely killing something. Jack kept tilting his head from side to side, ears very erect, and yet still could not understand what he was looking at. Jack could see a plastic Christmas cracker, which was of no interest, but could hear a squeaking and because Rowan was so intent on his business, Jack was positive that an animal must be involved. Where was it though? Poor Jack. I felt so sorry for his confusion. Most things I could help him understand. This I wasn't able to.

Before we left, Jack finally gave up trying to get to the bottom of this puzzle and ignored Rowan's activities, while we sat for the prize draw of the raffle. The prizes were laid out on a table and when a person's number was called, they stepped up and chose what suited them. After three of our numbers were called, we went home with our favourite sparkling, herbal fruit drink to have with our pasta, that evening.

Jack loved pasta, especially with my homemade tomato sauce or pesto and Parmesan and the pasta was always whole-wheat fusilli spirals. Unable to buy any fusilli, we had to use some whole-wheat pasta shells instead. The bowls were disgustingly full, which meant I always left some for Jack. And he knew it, sleeping in his bed until 'the sign' – my sleeves being pushed up beyond my elbows. Up Jack would leap, waving his tail about, ears up, (they were always up, even when asleep!) eyes shining eagerly.

First, I would open the door to the kitchen and switch on the light, then carrying both bowls, would walk into the kitchen. Jack knew to keep just behind my leg, although, if the excitement got too much, propelling him forward into the kitchen, ahead of me, back I would turn, into the living room. "Get back here now," I would say, not in a nasty way but in a firm tone. In Jack would rush, in frantic impatience, positioning himself behind me. Once more we would set off into the kitchen, this time with Jack dancing two to the dozen to heel, like a horse being held back from flying off. Why couldn't he be so obedient in the woods? A couple of feet over the threshold, Jack could then rush round into place, eyes popping out of his head, tasting the food already in his mind, while I tipped the pasta into one bowl. "Sit," I demanded. It was a half-sit, due to Jack's sore back, and he told me so. "All right," I said, "If it hurts, you don't have to sit properly."

I placed the bowl into Jack's own bowl. As he hastened to grab a mouthful, Jack abruptly stopped and stared. "What is it lovey?" I queried. He sniffed the pasta. I realised. "It's all right, it's still pasta, it's just a different shape that's all. It tastes the same." Tentatively, Jack picked up a shell and chewed carefully. "Mmm, so it does." Gobble, gobble, gobble. It had never occurred to me that Jack had noticed the particular shape of the food he was eating. In a way, I wasn't surprised because this typified Jack – he noticed fine detail and small changes. In fact he noticed everything – you couldn't fool Jack.

We had hung a new bird feeder in our mulberry tree and on the same day, the first time Jack went out into the garden, it caught his eye. Mark and I both watched as Jack looked up and studied it for a while. "Might have known he'd spot it straight away," said Mark.

On a different date, Mark and I fitted a couple of domestic smoke alarms; one in the dining room, the other in the living room, both fixed to the ceiling. That evening, as Jack was lying on his duvet in the dining room, propped on his elbow, whilst I brushed his teeth with his poultry-flavour toothpaste, he pointed his head upwards in an effort to lick the toothpaste off the brush. Normally, his eyes were half closed, while this activity took place but at this moment, his eyes widened, as he stared at the ceiling. "What is he looking at?" I thought, following his gaze. The smoke alarm – I should have known! "It's a smoke alarm," I explained. He accepted this answer and brought his head down again.

Although Mark was called Mark and Jack's name was Jack and they both knew this, I more often called each of them 'lovey', as a term of endearment. It must be my age!

This did cause confusion on a couple of occasions, when I called out the word. After our evening shower, Mark was still in the bathroom, cleaning up. Jack was in his bed in the bedroom. Being ready to go down to start the tea, I called out to Mark, "I'm going down now lovey." "O.k." said Mark, just as Jack rushed onto the landing, tail in the air, ready to step onto the stairs, looking at me as if to say, "Right Mummy, here I am." "Oh!" I exclaimed, "I was talking to Daddy but that's o.k. Shall we go down?" "Yes," Jack acquiesced and down we tripped together. "Slowly, slowly," I said, pointing to the stairs, so that Jack didn't rush ahead and jump from high up, which he sometimes did in excitement.

The other time, Mark and Jack were in the living room and I was in the kitchen. "Lovey?" I called to Mark to get his attention, ready to ask him a question. Jack shot into the kitchen, "Yes Mummy. Where's the food then?" "Ah lovey," I said, cuddling him, "I was calling Daddy. I call you both lovey. I'm sorry to confuse you. You're such a good boy."

Whether Jack knew the difference between the words 'lovey' and 'lovely', I'm not sure. He certainly heard them a lot. I was constantly telling him, "Ooo, you are lovely," especially when relaxing in his big bed, on his back; legs in the air, head back, mouth slightly gaping, occasionally snoring softly. So as not to shock him into leaping up in self-defence, I would kneel by his bed and say, "Hello Jack." The visible eye, would half open to survey me with that casual, "Oh, it's only you," look, then close again. His chest would expand and a long sigh of contentment escape, as he waited for the worship and adoration to begin.

"What a lovely tummy you've got. Look at that tummy," I would say, planting many kisses on Jack's chest. "Oh, it's lovely," kiss, kiss, kiss, and the odd raspberry would be blown against it. I would stroke his shoulders, legs, neck and play with his feet, telling him, "What beautiful feet you have," and he loved every minute of it.

Quite often, when Jack was resting on his elbow and had requested the pleasure of my company by his bed and I had put my arms around him, I would close my eyes, as did Jack likewise, and run my hands over every inch of his body, to almost imprint it on my mind. I removed the sense of looking with my eyes, to concentrate fully on what I felt through my hands. The difference between the soft short fur of his ears to the long, coarser hair of his tail. The soft fur on his neck was dense compared to the short, soft hair covering his shoulder muscles. The fur along the top of his back was silky, with longer guard hairs. All his fur was soft, like silk-velvet. I loved the feel of each muscle group and how defined they were. Like a blind person, I would feel the shape of his front legs, rear legs, feet, chest, neck, head, face and all along his back. I loved every bit of Jack, right down to the tiniest hairs on his chin.

Not only did I love to touch Jack, I loved to watch Jack. On a pleasant spring day, sun shining, not too hot, not too cold, Jack would ask to be let into the garden to lie by his bushes. Outside, Jack never flaked out flat. No. He only ever lay like Anubis, when watching Mark or I, or when on his own, lay propped on one elbow by the said bushes, to survey his garden through half-closed eyes.

He was clearly visible from the kitchen or landing window and I would watch him, without him knowing. Lying in quiet repose, he contemplated everything in the garden – the birds fluttering around the feeders, the birds pecking around on the floor, quite close to Jack at times yet in complete safety. The butterflies, the long grass waving in the breeze. Various scents wafting across to him would send Jack's nose a little higher, as he sniffed, then back down. Even squirrels that dared trespass were regarded with composure. There was no point in going after prey, which knew exactly where he was and nor did he want to disturb his restful serenity.

There were times when Jack's eyes actually closed, as if dozing and periodically his head would nod but not for long. I suspected Jack was worried that a fly may land on him. More than five flies, one after the other, would bring him to the back door, wanting to come in.

One warm, sunny day, I had been sitting on the lawn, with my back against a large log, when Jack came to lay by me. After stroking him and holding his paw, I had to go into the house, so Jack got up too and went to lie by his bushes. As I looked up from my work in the kitchen, I saw Jack get up and go to lie where I had previously been sitting. Did he feel closer to me by doing that?

Maybe Jack viewed these times as non-hunting times, unlike if he was in the house lying in his big bed and I, observing about six pesky squirrels through the kitchen window, would whisper, "Squirrel in the garden." Jack was at the back door in a flash, whining with impatience. A quiet, "Ssh," from me, would silence him into seriousness. Opening the door quietly, I would let Jack out to slip surreptitiously up the steps. By now, it was the beginning of April and our long grass areas were far too short to hide Jack from the squirrel's eyes. Seeing him in hunt-mode, they leisurely made themselves scarce.

Instead of waiting for rabbits to come to him, Jack told us in no uncertain terms, that as the evenings lengthened, he wanted to look around the orangery, to see if any could be caught out. I was hoping there wouldn't be any rabbits out, one evening, but there were, three of which Jack chased, all escaping capture. Jack did graze the back of one of his front feet, as he ran off the grass and pulled up on the gravel path. I'm sure he stopped so abruptly where he wouldn't normally do so, due to pain.

The next evening, Jack requested a walk down to the orangery. I didn't really want to go, yet I didn't want to disappoint Jack. I worried about the future. Would he always persist in hunting rabbits? Very probably.

Round the back we walked – not a rabbit to be seen. Mark went round to the left, while Jack and I went to the right, to meet round the front of the building. I could see Mark standing at the far side, pointing. Following where he indicated, with my eyes, there on the croquet lawn, was a large rabbit trying its best to flatten itself to the ground. Jack, who had also stopped, now noticed the cringing rabbit. I wasn't close enough to get hold of his collar and if I called out, the rabbit might run, causing Jack to run.

Mark and I kept quiet and watched as Jack slowly walked forward. Keeping the same pace, he reached the rabbit, which unexpectedly, leapt three feet in the air vertically, in the hope of surprising Jack. Like lightening, Jack snapped the rabbit out of the air and ran past me, to bury it behind the orangery. I was rendered speechless. Mark whooped out and afterwards, we couldn't stop talking about it. "Did you see that?" panted Mark to me. "That was amazing. That rabbit must have fooled the cat like that but met its match with Jack," I said excitedly back. "Cool as a cucumber; he never jumped; just grabbed it out of the air. I've never seen anything like it!" Mark gabbled on. "If he caught them all like that, he wouldn't hurt himself," I remarked wryly.

The squeaking started again when Jack lifted and lowered his head. I contacted our vet and asked him to recommend a dog physiotherapist. He put me in touch with a young lady with magical hands.

After a thorough examination, with Jack being 'lunged' like a horse, then lots of probing, which Jack objected to, some manipulation was applied. Jack was very well behaved, putting up with all the pain, as old racing injuries were dredged up. After around a couple of hours, he got a bit grouchy, and who could blame him?

The physio requested x-rays to be taken of Jack's lower cervical/thoracic spine and the lumbo-sacral junction. That evening, Jack's whole demeanour was much brighter, as if a weight had been lifted from his shoulders and his mind. Just one treatment had made a huge difference. As instructed by the physio, I massaged Jack three times a day, the way she had shown me and gave him a low dose of Rimadyl.

One week later, we took Jack for his x-rays. Unfortunately, no one had said to starve him, so I had given him his breakfast. "We can't do it," the nurse said. "Well, I'm not coming back another day. I've taken time off work to come here," Mark said determinedly. "Why didn't anyone say to starve him?" I asked. "You should know," came the reply. After much to-ing and fro-ing, the vet was brought through. "Can you keep him until he's digested his food, then do it?" I asked. "Yes, we could but it won't be very nice for Jack. It means he'll be here all day," he said. "I know but we need the x-rays today, to be able to take them to the physio tomorrow," I explained. It was finally agreed and Mark and I left as Jack was walked through a door, to his kennel. A whole day without Jack – horrible. I hated leaving him.

Keeping to my routine, which was now a late morning walk, I went out at the usual time, round the wood, thinking about Jack the whole time. It was a lovely sunny day, which made me feel bad that Jack was cooped up indoors. Along one of the trails, a large sweet chestnut bough barred the way, where it had fallen during the night. Having to climb through its branches, I thought to myself that if Jack had been with me, we would have had to have gone another route. When I reached home, I telephoned the wood yard to report the fallen bough, then thought no more of it.

Lunchtime was strange without Jack to share my sandwiches. Mark found it strange too, although he had his work to keep him occupied, whilst I, who shared every moment with Jack, had to get through the afternoon, which seemed to stretch out in front of me.

When Mark finished work, we went straight to pick Jack up, who was still very sleepy. Making sure I didn't forget the x-rays, I sat in the back of the Land Rover to steady Jack, as he always insisted on standing up and wavering about, after an anaesthetic.

The following morning, it was lovely to have Jack with me on our woodland walk. Forgetting about the fallen bough, I unwittingly took Jack towards the blocked track. As we rounded the corner together, I suddenly remembered. Then I saw that the obstruction had been cleared away. What astounded me was Jack's reaction. As he trotted over where the bough had rested, he stopped abruptly, looked at the floor, walked back and to, then glanced between the trees at the edge of the path. Immediately, he spotted the correct bough, where the wood yard had left it after dragging it off the track, and lost no time in going to examine it in great detail. I have never before, met a dog who would notice such things. But then, Jack was different.

That evening was Jack's second appointment with the physio, for deep work and a time on the Tens machine. Jack seemed to enjoy this visit far more, nearly falling asleep. I was shown how to stretch the muscles and how to work each area, being told to work for ten minutes on the neck and shoulders and a further ten minutes on the lumbo-sacral junction. Jack went home a happy dog.

Three times a day, after walks, I would get Jack to lie on his duvet, while I gave him his massage. He was so relaxed that he was extremely reluctant to get up and lie the opposite way, so that I could work on his other side. It took a lot of persuasion on my part!

All this treatment worked wonders. Jack became more animated on his walks, having an early morning burn-up now and again. So he hadn't been slowing down due to being more calm. It had been because he was in pain and discomfort. I was so happy for him and decided not to take him round the orangery, in the future.

Our next physio appointment should have been in two weeks time, on a Tuesday, but due to the Land Rover having to go in that day for a new clutch and work on the back axle, it was agreed I would telephone to make another date, when convenient. Meanwhile, I carried on with Jack's treatment. The new clutch was fitted and much to our relief, our trusty Land Rover was back on the road, running smoothly.

A couple of days later, apologising to Jack, I popped to Gill and Henry's, next door for one hour, to their coffee morning, which they always held in May to raise money for flowers for the church. The hour went by and I said my goodbyes, returning home laden with fruitcake for Mark and lemon curd, which I found Mark is not keen on!

"I'm sorry Jack lovey," I told a slightly worried Jack, "We'll go our walk now. I'll just go and get changed. I won't be a minute," and I rushed upstairs. A change of trousers, a wee and then into the bathroom to wash my hands. I glanced into the mirror above the basin. Suddenly, words seemed to come into my head or just by my head, "I'm going to take Jack." "No, don't take him. Please don't take him," I said, bursting into tears.

Quickly, I told myself that I had a vivid imagination and not to be so stupid. Drying my eyes and re-applying moisturiser, I put it out of my head, going down to put my Wellingtons on and take Jack out. The weather alternated between sun and cloud and it was pleasant in the wood, Jack no longer plodding behind, but his usual cheeky self.

Being a Thursday meant that when Mark came home from work, he had to go shopping. Jack did not want him to go, which was unusual. While Mark was out, I noticed a baby rabbit at the bottom of the garden, which didn't look well. When I opened the back door, Jack went out and walked carefully towards the rabbit. It was not aware of him even as he stood over it. One bite and it was dead. Jack then buried it in the compost heap.

Just at that moment, Mark arrived with the shopping. When Mark walked into the garden, Jack retrieved his rabbit to show him, then decided to lie down and eat it, all the while that Mark was back and to with bags of groceries. Once in the house, Jack wanted Mark to hug him. He was very insistent on it, which was unusual.

Friday had been a perfectly normal day, apart from the afternoon. Mark finished work early, so we went into town to buy an off-cut of carpet to fit in the cubby-hole, in the kitchen. As usual, Mark wanted to get the job done as soon as we got home. Jack supervised, as he always did, lying in the kitchen and placing his paw on the new carpet, as Mark cut it to size. It took far longer than anticipated, but looked lovely when finished.

The day ended with Mark and Jack walking down to the church, as usual. Just as we were going upstairs to bed, I noticed that Jack looked as though he was trying to eject something from his mouth, using his tongue. I suspected one of my long hairs. Opening his jaws, I peered down his throat. No sign of any hair or anything else. Whatever it was would sort itself out or become apparent. We climbed into bed about ten p.m. and soon fell asleep.

An hour later, I was woken by Jack bringing up everything he had eaten over the last few hours. "Oh no," I thought, as I put the lamp on and got out of bed in my pyjamas. Another lot came up. Both piles were on the Chinese wool rug – lovely! I went down for a bucket of soapy water and disinfectant, newspaper, gloves and a cloth. After cleaning up, down I went to wash the bucket and cloth out and put the sick in the bin outside.

Well, at least he's got rid of whatever it was. Now we can all get back to sleep. No sooner was my head on the pillow, then Jack was vomiting again – this time yellow bile. Fetching my bucket, paper, gloves and cloth again, I cleared up once more. Jack kept on heaving and producing yellow froth. Mark was also up by now. "Shut all the doors, so he stays on the landing," I instructed, to make my job of cleaning up easier.

By two twenty-five a.m. the next morning, we were all exhausted. Whilst I was downstairs getting fresh soapy water, I realised something was not right and phoned the emergency vet. Please let it be ours, I prayed. A very sleepy, familiar voice answered. Thank goodness. "It's Jack," I told him, "He just keeps being sick. He started just gone ten, last night when he brought up all his food. Now it's just bile." "Bring him in. I'll meet you in half an hour," he said. "Mark," I called, "We're taking Jack to the vets.

Come on let's get going." Throwing our clothes on, we were soon in the Land Rover, speeding along quiet roads, with me sitting in the back to supervise Jack.

We arrived just before the vet. "Has he been poisoned?" I asked directly. "No," said the vet, looking quite shocked. "What's he eaten?" he asked. Feeling a little ashamed to admit it, I said I'd given him a piece of garlic bread, at tea time, but apart from that, just his normal food, which I listed. "Could it be parvo or enteritis?" I queried. "Doesn't really look like either of those," the vet pondered. "If he dies, I want to take him home," I suddenly stated. "He's not going to die," gasped the vet, staring at me as if I was mad. He said it could be from Jack's stomach or it could be his brain telling him to vomit for no reason, which would be his central nervous system. After giving Jack an injection of anti-emetic, we were told to go home and if the sickness didn't stop after two hours, to ring him again.

I felt awful having to take Jack back home, still being sick. "We'll sleep downstairs with him," I told a reluctant Mark. "You get your sleeping bag and my aerobics mat and put it on the living room floor. I'll sleep on the settee because of my back." "All right then," Mark agreed. Well, I hardly touched the settee. Jack trampled all over Mark, continued vomiting all over the kitchen, dining room and cubby-hole, finally ending up trying to scrape everything out of his way, in the cubby-hole – the sacks of bird grain and his biscuit meal – to reach the back, which is only twelve inches high.

I could have wept to see him in such a desperate state. I couldn't imagine his suffering. Looking at my watch, I realised two hours had gone by, with no improvement. Worried, I phoned the vet. "He's not stopped," I said. "I'll meet you at the surgery in half an hour," he said. "Right Mark. Get up, we've got to take Jack in again," I called.

It was like déjà vu, as we drove along feeling shattered, our stomachs in knots. By now Jack was seriously dehydrated and was put on a drip, straight away. The vet said he would ring after they had performed some tests. We went home feeling quite empty.

At eight a.m. the vet rang to say Jack's heart rate was high, he had a high temperature, had blood tests and x-rays, which revealed nothing, had continued to be sick three more times and was salivating a great deal. We sat indoors, waiting for more news and waiting for our visiting time of twelve thirty p.m. It seemed an age until that time came around, yet it did.

Jack looked so much better and was exceptionally pleased to see us, which was a joy to us, as normally he didn't show us much emotion whenever we picked him up from the vets - he usually wanted to be with the other dogs. This time, we were his main focus and I'd never seen him so glad that we were there. This meant an awful lot to Mark and I. The head nurse and another nurse were just about to carry out some tests or cleaning on Jack, which meant we had to leave but we made sure we arranged to come back later. Seeing him looking so well, gave us confidence enough to go and do our Saturday shopping and even go a walk around the estate.

We visited Jack at four thirty p.m. to find him lying quietly in his kennel. The vet on duty, who was new to the practice, reported that he had only been sick once since lunchtime. Straight away, I could see that he was not as well as he had been. We were handed his drip and allowed to walk him outside, for a wee. Once outside, Jack looked over at the Land Rover and I could see his cheeky look, as if to say, "I'm not going in there yet," and he took us in the opposite direction. Watching him walk brought a lump to my throat and when he cocked his leg, it was with great difficulty. His legs shook uncontrollably with weakness. My poor Jack. "We'd better take him in before he collapses," I told Mark. Jack didn't mind entering the waiting room but refused to walk up the corridor to the kennels. The vet came along, saying, "He always does this," positioning herself behind Jack and pushing him along. Normally, Jack would have loved going to the kennels to be with the other dogs. Not this time. The three of us managed to get him into the kennel and onto his bedding. The vet left us with Jack, who started to shake violently and pant furiously, eyes staring wildly, his whole body rigid. I rushed to get the vet. "Oh no, that's what he always does. It's normal," she replied to my worried questions. "It doesn't look normal," I commented. Mark had turned Jack round and I knelt down and held him. The full weight of his body was leaning on me, when he suddenly emptied his bladder all over my leg. That wasn't like Jack, at all. The look of puzzled concern, which spread across the vets face, did not escape my notice, as she turned to leave the kennels. "I can't hold him anymore," I said to Mark, as my strength ebbed, "Help me lay him down." Between us, we laid Jack on his side and he calmed down. He lay as if asleep, sighing now and again. We sat for one hour, talking to him and stroking him. "We'd better leave him to sleep," I said wearily, "We'll come back later." Mark and I closed and bolted the kennel door. I was surprised when Jack didn't open his eyes and lift his head, to say, "Don't go without me." He never moved. We arranged with the vet to return at nine p.m.

Eating any food was well nigh impossible. We just felt ill, counting the hours and minutes until eight thirty p.m. when we could set off again. "It's a good job we had the clutch done before this happened," said Mark. "Things happen the way they're supposed to," I told him.

As we entered the surgery, the vet spoke in hushed tones, "He's not so good. He's been fitting for twenty minutes. I'm waiting for the head nurse so we can sedate him. You can come down and see him." Feeling quite numb, we crouched by him as he had his seizure. "You'd better go and sit in the waiting room for now," she told us, as the nurse arrived to get things underway.

Mark and I sat in silence, not knowing what to think yet never giving up hope. Once stabilised on Valium, we were allowed to see him. It was explained that during his fit he had lost control of his bladder and bowel, his diarrhoea containing a lot of blood. The vet suspected poison and said his prospects weren't good. The only good point was Jack's strong heart beat.

We were running on empty. Everything we did was mechanical. Our minds were in another place. We just went to bed and tried to sleep to shut this nightmare out.

I awoke very early and had to get up, waiting as long as I could before ringing the surgery. At seven a.m. I spoke to the vet. Jack had not come out of the Valium. She said she would ring again, which she did – at eleven a.m. and one p.m. to report no change. He should have woken by now, as he had not had a large dose of sedative.

I rang Anne Finch of Greyhounds in NEED, for her opinion. It was while talking to her about all Jack's symptoms, that it hit me that he must have started by having small fits throughout Saturday and he had a larger one whilst we were there, when he emptied his bladder on my leg. We talked about various poisons, in an effort to work out what was affecting Jack. After wearing her out, I said goodbye, feeling quite desolate.

Not being able to wait any longer, I phoned the vet and told her we were coming anyway. Arriving at two p.m. we sat by Jack's side, talking to him and caressing his soft fur. For a long time, Jack was comatose. After a couple of hours, we saw signs of life. His eyes were trying to open. His tongue was so dry, I requested a dish of water so that I could dampen it, which made Jack swallow and lick his mouth. The more conscious Jack became, he began to paddle his feet and bark wildly. "He's getting too stressed," the vet said, "I'll have to keep him sedated." This disappointed us. We left at five forty p.m. with Jack once more, asleep.

Trying to eat was impossible. A couple of mouths full was the maximum before I felt I would be sick. My stomach felt as though someone had twisted it round, many times.

Returning at nine p.m. to sit with Jack didn't really make us feel any better but we felt we had to be with him as much as possible. Periodically, Jack would start howling and barking, only quietening down when his bladder emptied. While we were there, we helped to change his bedding, turn him and cover him with a fresh towel. I had also brought his duvet cover and a pair of my trousers to lay by his head, so he could smell familiar scents. The anti-emetic drip was turned off, as there was now no need for it.

Nothing seemed real anymore, as we automatically made our way home at ten thirty p.m. to an empty house. We slept out of sheer fatigue. During the night, I woke from what appeared to be a dream – I saw Jack lying on his left side, not breathing. Then I abruptly woke up. Pushing it out of my head, I must have fallen asleep again, only to be brought out of it by the alarm, at five fifty a.m.

Knowing we could not visit Jack so early because it was a Monday and the surgery would be open as usual, was agony. They put us off until nine thirty a.m. and once there, wanted time before they allowed us to the kennels. I would not accept that. They submitted and Mark and I walked, as if in a dream, down that long corridor.

The head nurse, who was wonderful, was bathing Jack. An orthopaedic mattress had replaced the previous bedding, clean vet-fleece was laid on top with Jack gently positioned, before being covered with a blanket. Further tests had shown his blood, heart rate, strength of heartbeat, temperature and breathing to be normal. Jack had been taken off the Valium and put on a low dose of anaesthetic, at 18ml per hour, which was reduced to 6ml per hour when that syringe was empty. Our own vet was in and came to discuss everything that was done to Jack. Each time Jack started to come round, he would lift his head, barking wildly, panting, getting very hot, eyes staring, not seeing anyone. It was very distressing to witness.

A catheter was fitted to Jack's bladder to prevent his bedding getting soaked. One of his front paws had swollen through continual lying down. The head nurse kindly put a pressure bandage round it, whilst we massaged Jack's other feet. Mark and I talked – to Jack and about Jack, until at one thirty p.m. we thought it best to go home for a while.

Another morsel of food was painfully swallowed. We couldn't do anything. We couldn't walk; we couldn't read. We sat in front of the television, not really concentrating at all. As evening approached, we ate a tiny amount of food before our journey to the surgery.

Six p.m. and no change in Jack. A baby monitor had now been attached to the kennel door, to alert the staff of any sound Jack made. All of Jack's paws had swollen, including one hock and his urine showed liver damage. Our vet phoned DEFRA twice about testing for poisons but they informed him that it would be impossible to test for something when they didn't know what they were looking for. Our hearts sank.

The other head vet also came to discuss the situation and we all racked our brains. Mark and I had already asked our neighbour, Gill, if she used slug pellets but she never used them. In fact, she used no poisons at all. Rat bait-boxes were no longer used and hadn't been for some months. The pest-control man had not been round the back of our garden at all – the only thing he had done on the estate, was to bait mole runs in the meadow and walled garden. I knew Jack had not done anything unusual in the woods, while on our last walks, so what on earth was it?

Wearily, we made our way home at eight p.m. to have a very early night. I fell into a deep sleep, not waking until the alarm. Our vet had told us that we could be there at nine a.m. and we were taken straight down to Jack's kennel. As soon as I saw the catheter bag, I said, "His liver's worse." "Yes," said our vet, referring to the dark brown urine filling the bag. Mark and I sat with Jack for a while, wiping our eyes and blowing our noses on already sodden hankies, telling him how much we loved him and reciting to each other how amazing he was. Our vet came to tell us his thoughts. "I'd like to bring Jack out of the anaesthetic and see what happens. If he continues to bark and stare, I really don't think there's much hope. I think he's probably got brain damage." We agreed tearfully. "Would you like to wait in the Land Rover and I'll come and get you when I've decided?" he asked us. "Yes o.k." I said, "Don't put him down until we're here will you?" "No, I won't. I'll come and get you," he said.

Mark and I went outside and climbed into the Land Rover. The sun streamed in through the windows, warming everything but it didn't mean anything. After about half an hour, the vet appeared. "Is it time?" I asked. "Yes," he replied. "Right, let's do it," I said, and we strode quickly in through the back door. I could hear Jack's barking, as we approached the kennel room. We were soon by his side. I knelt down, stroking Jack, while poor Mark stood behind. There was only enough for the vet, as Jack had his head towards us.

As Jack paddled wildly with his paws, the vet had great difficulty in locating the syringe into the attachment, which was already taped to Jack's leg. How easily he could have been stabbed himself. He managed it in the end and as the barking stopped and the feet slowed, blinded by tears, I cradled Jack's head in my hands, telling him, "Bye, bye Jack. I love you. Bye, bye Jack," as he slipped quietly away.

CHAPTER 13

Afterwards

The vet left us. I asked the head nurse to remove all the drips and bandages and to put Jack into one of their large polythene bags, so that we could take him home. While she was doing this, I realised that Jack was lying on his left side, just as he had been in my dream. I felt empty yet relieved that the not knowing was over.

As soon as Jack was free of all his appendages, Mark and the head nurse manoeuvred him into the bag. The bag was then slid onto a large folded blanket, whereupon Mark, the vet and the head nurse carried Jack slung between them, out of the back door and into the Land Rover. "What about the money?" I asked the vet. "Don't bother now. Sort it out later, when you feel like it," he replied. The nurse hugged us and our vet was so upset – "What a waste," he kept saying. I think he was so shocked at the outcome, especially as Jack was only seven and a half years old. He always used to comment, when Jack visited, "He's such a fit dog. He just looks so fit," which made us feel good. We must have been doing something right. Thanking him and the nurse, we set off home, glad to have Jack with us.

Carrying Jack from the Land Rover across the garden, down the steps and into the house, I was not expecting him to be so heavy. We left him in the kitchen, still in the bag, on the blanket and changed into our work clothes, then fetching the correct tools, discussed where to site the grave. Our decision was unanimous – where Jack used to lie in the shade of his bushes. Between us, we carried Jack in the bag, out onto the lawn, so that I could measure how wide the hole should be.

Mark, being the expert, lifted the turf. Wanting to contribute in some way, I volunteered to dig the first foot and did so without too much trouble. "You'll have to do it now," I said, handing the spade to Mark. From there on the soil was full of rubble, bricks, glass, pottery, pig bones, tiles and flints! Poor Mark. What hard work.

When the hole was up to Mark's armpits and three feet by three feet, it looked very professional. I ran to get Jack's duvet cover. Laying it out on the lawn, we carefully extracted Jack from the bag and put him in the centre of the cover. He smelt strongly of anaesthetic and urine.

With great difficulty on my part, we lowered Jack into his grave. Mark then climbed in to wrap him up, only leaving his head showing for now. I handed Mark some of Jack's biscuit meal, his favourite black Bonio, a small rawhide chew and a small tub of water, which he placed by Jack's head.

Gill, from next door, came round and put a flower into the grave. We all said a few words before Mark, very carefully, began to pack the soil around Jack, once he had folded the duvet cover over Jack's face. We talked until all the earth was back in the hole, when we said goodbye to Gill. The turf was left off, as we had decided to plant a native tree on the grave. Our eyes puffy and swollen through crying so much, we both carried an empty ache inside and had both lost four or five pounds in weight.

Mark was given another day off work and we went to a tree nursery to choose a tree. A field maple was deemed suitable, as it would not grow too big. The one we picked wasn't very tall yet as I sat holding it in the Land Rover, it only just fitted in. Mark planted it, re-laying the turf and watering in. Over the next few days rain fell, which saved us the job of any further watering.

Mark went back to work, which occupied him and stopped him thinking too much. I was at home all day and every moment, Jack was in my thoughts. Although I coped well, many tears were shed and I missed Jack terribly. It was especially hard when meeting all the dog-walkers that Jack and I knew, when I went our normal walk. All my explanations ended with my eyes brimming and quite often theirs too, as Jack had been esteemed by many. It brought it home to me just how many people and dogs I had met through Jack. Our mantles and shelves overflowed with cards from these friends.

Three days after Jack's burial, Mark said he could smell anaesthetic in the living room doorway, where Jack used to lie watching us, when we were in the kitchen. "It can't be," I said, "We never put him in there and I washed the blanket straight away, then it went back to the vets." "Well there's a smell there," he reiterated. I went and stood where Jack used to lie. Yes, there was a smell of anaesthetic but only in that area – nowhere else. "It must be Jack," was all I could say.

Over the next two weeks, I smelt the same smell in various parts of the house, at different times. In the office, bathroom, dining room, kitchen, on the stairs and Mark smelt it sometimes in the cubby-hole. One day, while on my walk, I smelt it twice in the wood.

After the two weeks, the smell was more of urine and not as frequent. I feel Jack's presence very strongly in the house, garden and wood. In fact, the place he considered his home and where he obviously loved very much.

Even now, many months later, I still smell Jack at odd times, around the house and his basket has started to creak occasionally. As it stands on a concrete floor, there can be no movement of wooden floorboards to affect it – I keep an open mind about this.

Many are the times that I have found it hard to believe that Jack has gone. When he was alive, I couldn't bear to contemplate what life would be like if anything happened to him. And now I know. Like in W.H. Auden's 'Funeral Blues', 'He was my North, my South, my East and West' but unlike his poem, the stars are wanted, along with the moon and the sun, and so are the oceans and the wood, for I see Jack in all of them.

One of my favourite photo's of Jack if of him lying on the lawn, in the manner of Anubis, staring straight through the camera and right into me – this typifies Jack – cool, calm, collected, composed and in control. Discerning, perspicacious, self-assured. He had poise, great dignity and integrity. He had a great presence, which humbled many people and dogs. Yes, he could be perverse and demanding but that was a part of him, which probably made me love him even more. He had hidden depths too; depths I couldn't quite fathom – he was very deep.

When I explained to people that Jack had been special, they misunderstood what I meant, thinking that all our pets are special in their own way. Jack was truly special because he was so different – he was unique. Once he was made, the mould was broken. There will never be another like Jack. He had the X-factor.

How I miss hearing Jack's voice and holding him and feeling his soft fur. If I close my eyes, I can almost experience the sensation of my hands on his fur, when I used to sit by him, exploring every inch, as a blind person.

Looking through copies of Jack's racing papers, it shook me to read that the date of his last race was only four days before we picked him up, and not ten days, as we had been told.

As time has gone on, I have deliberated on how Jack died, coming to the conclusion that he could not have been poisoned and that his death was through natural causes. There being no poison for himself or another animal to pick up, is one indication that he did not ingest poison. No other dog or animal became ill or died with the same symptoms. The baby rabbit he ate on the previous day to his sickness could not have been poisoned, as no poisons were used. Although the rabbit was not well, it is a well-known fact that predators will prey on sick animals and consume them with no ill effects whatsoever. Both Mark and I were always with him and knew his every movement. My mind has gone back to my premonitions that Jack would not live to old age and that something in his head would go wrong. It was his central nervous system that was affected and coupled with the fact that his immune system had a fault, I suspect that this end was building up like a time bomb, ready to go off without warning.

My thoughts have also dwelt on my becoming quite paranoid about Jack's safety, the closer his fore coming death became. I refused to leave him in the Land Rover and preferred to stay by his side at every opportunity. My anxiety levels soared. I had noticed that Jack was distressed when Mark went shopping whereas previously, as long as I was there, he couldn't care less. He made it clear that he did not want Mark to go. He wanted us all to be together.

I am so very glad that Mark and I both, allowed Jack to live the life he wanted. The one that suited him. He always reminded me of a wolf. Such natural instincts and so well executed. How he loved hunting rabbits and squirrels, and his sense of achievement when successful. Understanding Jack so well, I knew that if we had prevented his hunting, he would have led a very frustrated and unhappy life. Now he has gone, I can look back knowing we did the right thing in accepting Jack as he was and I am so very glad that I told him how much I loved him – I have nothing to feel guilty about.

The only thing that remains to be said is that it has been a great honour and an even greater privilege to have shared Jack's life in his retirement, no matter how short. He brought me much joy and laughter and will be remembered and esteemed for the rest of my life.

THE END

Postscript

Since finishing the book, the vet's diagnosis of Jack's symptoms as poisoning, still rankled in my mind. It didn't add up. Mark and I frequently talked it over, combing through our memories and raking out anything that could be apposite.

It was on one of these occasions that Mark pointed to Jack's flea shampoo. With a feeling of disquiet, I read the active ingredient – Permethrin. What was this and was it dangerous?

After some research, I was able to ascertain that Permethrin is a toxic pesticide; is harmful if absorbed through the skin, the target organ being the central nervous system and can cause convulsions, ataxia and coma.

I have since come across other reports of the dangers of flea shampoos, containing chemicals, for dogs. Whether the shampoo was solely responsible for Jack's death or whether because his immune system was faulty and this made him more susceptible, I'll never know.

Now knowing that greyhounds are far more sensitive to chemicals than other dogs and bearing in mind the vet's prognosis, in future I will choose natural flea treatments for any greyhounds that share my life.

If I Knew

It is unclear who the author of this poem is. Three people claim authorship-
Copyright George Michael Grossman
Written by Joanie and Gena (a mother and daughter)